TOM PETERS
ESSENTIALS
TALENT

THE ESSENTIALS SERIES IS ADAPTED FROM *RE-IMAGINE!*

LONDON, NEW YORK, MUNICH,
MELBOURNE, AND DELHI

Editor **Michael Slind**
Project Art Editor **Jason Godfrey at Godfrey Design**
Senior Editor **Dawn Henderson**
DTP Design and Reproduction **Adam Walker**
Production Controller **Luca Frassinetti**
Managing Editor **Julie Oughton**
Managing Art Editor **Heather McCarry**
Publishing Manager **Adèle Hayward**
Category Publisher **Stephanie Jackson**
Art Director **Peter Luff**

First published in the USA in 2005 by
DK Publishing, Inc.
375 Hudson Street, New York, NY 10014

First published in Great Britain in 2005 by
Dorling Kindersley Limited,
80 Strand, London WC2R 0RL
A Penguin Company

2 4 6 8 10 9 7 5 3 1

DK books are available at special discounts for bulk purchases for sales promotions,
premiums, fund-raising, or educational use. For details contact: SpecialSales@dk.com

A Cataloging-in-Publication record for this book
is available from the Library of Congress.
(US) ISBN 0-7566-1056-7

A CIP catalog record for this book
is available from the British Library.
(UK) ISBN 1 4053 0260 7

Reproduced by Colourscan, Singapore
Printed and bound in Italy by Graphicom

Discover more at
www.dk.com

CONTENTS

INTRODUCTION

Re-imagining ... What's Essential

Fall 2003. I publish my Big Book ... *Business Excellence in a Disruptive Age*. It is, since the publication of *In Search of Excellence* in 1982, my most ambitious attempt to state comprehensively ... What Business Is. (Or Could Be.) (Or *Must* Be.)

The year following, 2004. While traveling to promote the book ... and while keeping up with my usual speaking and consulting schedule... I note a steadily increasing drumbeat. A drumbeat of consternation around the issue of "outsourcing." (Or "off-shoring.") Jobs going to India. Or China. Or just ... Somewhere Else.

What is to be done? How can people cope ... with the specter of ... massive job shrinkage? My (nutshell) answer: Job shrinkage is inevitable. Whether because of outsourcing or automation (which, long-term, may be a bigger deal than outsourcing), you can't count on any job being "there for you." What you can do is find ways to move yourself and your company Up the Value Chain ... and into the heart and soul of the New Economy.

Summer 2005. I publish a series of four quick and to-the-point books, one of which you now hold in your hand. The "Essentials" is what the series is called. As in: Here are the essential things you *must* know ... as you strive to *act* ... in this unstable, up-tempo, outsourcing-addled, out-of-this-world age.

New Economy, New Mandate, New Story

A lot of yogurt has hit the fan. In the near term, globalization continues to be a mixed blessing—a worthy end point, but messy and uneven to the extreme in its immediate impact. Waves of technological change engulf us—and confuse us. Corporate scandals erupt. Once-mighty titans (namely: big companies and the CEOs who lead them) fall from their lofty perches

And yet ... there *is* a New Economy.

Would you change places with your grandfather? Would you want to work 11 brutal hours a day ... in yesterday's Bethlehem Steel mill, or a Ford Motor Company factory circa 1935? Not me. Nor would I change places with my father ... who labored in a white-collar sweatshop, at the same company, in the same building, for 41 l-o-n-g years.

A workplace revolution is under way. No sensible person expects to spend a lifetime in a single corporation anymore. Some call this shift the "end of corporate responsibility." I call it ... the Beginning of Renewed Individual Responsibility. An extraordinary opportunity to take charge of our own lives.

Put me in charge! Make me Chairman and CEO and President and COO of Tom Inc.

That's what I ask! (Beg, in fact.)

I *love* business at its best. When it aims to foster growth and deliver exciting services to its clients and exciting opportunities to its employees. I especially *love* business at this moment of flux. This truly magical, albeit in many ways terrifying, moment.

I'm no Pollyanna. I've been around. (And then around.) My rose-colored glasses were long ago ground to powder by brutal reality.

Yet I am hopeful. Not hopeful that human beings will become more benign ... or that evil will evaporate ... or that greed will be regulated out of existence. But I am hopeful that in the New Economy people will see the power that comes from taking responsibility for their professional lives. And I am hopeful that they also will find pleasure in unleashing their instinctive curiosity and creativity.

The harsh news: This is Not Optional. The microchip will colonize all rote activities. And we will have to scramble to reinvent ourselves—as we did when we came off the farm and went into the factory, and then as we were ejected from the factory and delivered to the white-collar towers.

The exciting news (as I see it, anyway): This is Not Optional. The reinvented *you* and the reinvented *me* will have no choice but to scramble and add value in some meaningful way.

The Back-Story: A Tale/Trail of Disruption

Each book in the series builds on a central premise—the same premise that I propounded in the early chapters of *Re-imagine*! Herewith, an Executive Summary of that Progression of Ideas.

1. All bets are off. It is the foremost task—and responsibility—of our generation to re-imagine our enterprises and institutions, public and private. Rather strong rhetoric. But I believe it. The fundamental nature of the change now in progress has caught us off-stride and on our heels. No aspect of the way our institutions operate can be allowed to go unexamined. Or unchanged.

2. We are in a ... Brawl with No Rules. Business, politics, and, indeed, the essential nature of human interchange have come unglued. We have to make things up as we go along. (Success = SAV = "Screw Around Vigorously.") ("Fail. Forward. Fast.") Yesterday's strictures and structures leave us laughably—and tragically—unprepared for this Brawl with No Rules. From al Qaeda to Wal*Mart, new entrants on the world stage have flummoxed regnant institutions and their leaders.

3. Incrementalism is *Out*. Destruction is *In*. "Continuous improvement," the lead mantra of 1980s management, is now downright dangerous. All or nothing. ("Control. Alt. Delete.") We must gut the innards of our enterprises before new competitors do it for us—and to us.

4. InfoTech changes everything. There is no higher priority than the Total Transformation of all business practice to e-business practice. The new technologies are ... The Real Thing. The IT Revolution is in its infancy. And yet it has already changed the rules—changed them so fundamentally that years and years will pass before we can begin talking about constructing a new rule book.

5. Ninety percent of white-collar jobs as we know them (and, ultimately, 90 percent of all jobs as we know them) will be disemboweled in the next 15 years. Done. Gone. Kaput. Between the microprocessor, 60/60/24/7 connectivity, and outsourcing to developing countries, the developed nations' white-collar jobs are ... doomed. Time frame? Zero to 15 or 20 years. How confident am I on this point? Totally.

6. "Winners" (survivors!) will become *de facto* bosses of Me Inc. Self-reliance will, of necessity, replace corporate cosseting. Old-style corporate security is evaporating. Upshot: Free the cubicle slaves! The only defense is a good offense! Hackneyed? Sure. But no less true for being so. A scary ... but also immensely exciting ... New Age of Self-Reliance is being birthed before our eyes. Hurray!

Story Time—for a Storied Time

Building on that premise, each book in this series tells a story—a saga of how we will survive (and, perhaps, go beyond survival) in this Dizzy, Disruptive Age.

A Story about *Leadership*. Command-and-control management ... "leadership" from on high ... is obsolete. New Leadership draws on a new skill set—the hallmarks of which are improvisation and inspiration. It taps into the unique leadership attributes of women. It cultivates Great Talent by creating a Great Place to Work.

A Story about *Design*. New Value-Added derives less and less from "product" or "service" quality, and more and more from ... Something More. Something called "Experiences." Something called "Branding." Something called "Design."

A Story about *Talent*. It's a Brand You World. "Lifetime employment" at a corporation (aka "cubicle slavery") is out. Lifetime self-reinvention is in. The only fool-proof source of job security is … your talent. And your talent will express itself by building a scintillating portfolio of WOW Projects and by Thinking Weird (as these weird, wild times demand).

A Story about *Trends*. Where, amid so much flux and discontinuity, are the Big Market Opportunities? They are hiding in plain sight. Go where they buyers are and where the money is—among women and among aging boomers.

The Story Re-imagined: What's New

To tell these stories, I have adapted selected chapters from *Re-imagine!* As necessary or as I've seen fit, I have nipped and tucked and otherwise revised each chapter throughout. Plus, I have salted the tale here and there with new supporting material.

In addition, I—along with the folks at my publisher, Dorling Kindersley—have re-imagined the the look-and-feel of each book from the inside-out. With *Re-imagine!*, we set out to re-invent the business book. We wanted to tell the story of a world of enterprise that is bursting at the seams with revolutionary possibility, and so we created a book that bursts forth with Passion and Energy and Color. For the Essentials series, we have retained those qualities, but we have also stripped the design of these books down to its … essentials. Same Passion. Same Energy. Same Color. All in a format that fits in your hand … and meets (we believe) your essential needs.

Two new features punctuate and amplify the Story Being Told.

First, capping each chapter is a list of "Top 10 To-Dos"—a one-page digest of the chapter in the form of action items that will inspire you to Do Something … right away. Here again, the emphasis is on drilling down to … what's essential.

Second, between certain chapters we include highlights from interviews with "Cool Friends"—smart people whose work has helped make me smarter. Their voices add insights that give texture to the story. Full-text versions of these and other interviews appear on my Web site (www.tompeters.com).

Last Words ...

I don't expect you'll agree with everything that I say in this book. But I hope that when you disagree ... you will disagree *angrily*. That you will be so pissed off that you'll ... Do Something.

DOING SOMETHING. That's the essential idea, isn't it? The moral of my story—the story of What's Essential about the present moment in business—comes in the form of a tombstone. It's a tombstone that bears the epitaph that I most hope to avoid. To wit:

Thomas J. Peters
1942–Whenever
He would have done some really cool stuff ...
but his boss wouldn't let him

Meanwhile, I know exactly how I *do* want my tombstone to read:

Thomas J. Peters
1942–Whenever
HE WAS A PLAYER!

Not "He got rich." Not "He became famous." Not even "He got things right." Rather: "He was a player." In other words: He did *not* sit on the sidelines ... and watch the world go by ... as it was undergoing the most profound shift of basic premises in the last several hundred years (if not the last thousand years).

Agree or disagree with me on anything else, but if you have a grain of integrity or spirit or spunk or verve or nerve, you must agree with me on this: Getting off the sidelines—Being a Player—is Not Optional.

No. In fact, Being a Player is ... *Essential!*

1

Re-Imagining
the Individual:
Talent in a
Brand You World

Contrasts

Was	Is
Cubicle slavery	Free Agent Nation
Bland "unit"	Brand You!
Job for life	Gig for now
(Personnel file at Big Company)	(Portfolio of temporary assignments)
Benefits come from the company	Benefits travel with you through life
Career strategy: Do what you're told	Career strategy: Do what you excel at
Competence	Mastery
Reference group = The corporation	Reference group = Peers in my craft
The Detroit model: Punch in at the factory	The Hollywood model: Join a team at a studio
Work with the same old folks day in and day out	Work with a shifting network of partners
Goal: Become the boss (after 25 years)	Goal: Be the boss (now!)
Promotion on seniority	Getting gigs on merit
Work your way up "the ladder"	Leap your way across changing terrain
Vertical loyalty	Horizontal loyalty
Call the tech guy	Be the tech guy
Goal: Get through the day	Goal: Get things done
Know "the ropes"	Learn to bungee-jump!

!Rant

We are not prepared ...

WE KEEP TRYING (longing?) to veer back to the professional "career path" of old—**a model of employment in which Big Companies ruled** and we genuflected on command.

• **DAZZLED BY THE STILL ABIDING MYTH OF SECURITY, WE SHY AWAY FROM RECOGNIZING THAT NEW MODES OF ENTERPRISE REQUIRE NOTHING LESS THAN THE ...** *RE-IMAGINING OF THE INDIVIDUAL.* • Now we must take ... Immediate Charge ... of our new-fangled careers and identities—careers and identities that we will build piece by piece at a series of companies, small and large, over time. • **THAT'S SCARY.** • That's cool. • That's Life in a ... Brand You World.

!Vision

I imagine ...

A truly creative society: Each person moves from project to project, from gig to gig. • Global Voluntary Communities of Interest, rather than corporations, provide the bedrock upon which we stand. • **LEARNING NEVER CEASES. SELF-RELIANCE IS THE NORM. EACH CAREER CONSISTS OF NUMEROUS "MINI-CAREERS," WITH TIME-OUTS ALONG THE WAY.** (The cubicle slave is dead! **Long live the Free Agent!**) • People aren't just "people," and they certainly aren't just "employees." **PEOPLE ARE ... TALENT!** • And they, like their "bosses," recognize that *Talent Is All There Is.*

Talent Tale: My First "Pitch"

Labor Day 2000. My mother-in-law's 75th birthday. She said she had but a handful of Big Wishes. One of them: to attend a ballgame at Boston's fabled Fenway Park. So my brother-in-law took her, and my wife and I tagged along. We got lucky. Pedro Martinez was pitching for the Red Sox. He did what Pedro does. He made utter fools out of the nine talented athletes on the other team.

For me, it was a great day. I learned something: PEDRO MARTINEZ IS A BETTER BASEBALL PITCHER THAN I AM.

Not much of an insight, you say.

But I disagree.

FACT: Some people are more talented than other people.

FACT: Some people are a hell of a lot more talented than other people.

That's what I learned. And that's one of the Big Keys to the Talent Game.

Talent matters.

What is a "baseball team"? Simple: A baseball team is ... ITS ROSTER. Sports marketing is important. No doubt of it. But all the sports marketing in the world won't make up for a team that loses year after year. In the mid- to long-run, Talent Rules.

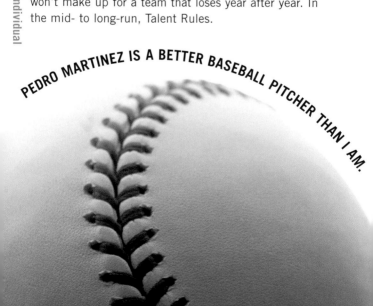

PEDRO MARTINEZ IS A BETTER BASEBALL PITCHER THAN I AM.

Talent (if you're serious about it) is a 25-8-53 affair

"Talent," the Term

Talent. I love that word!

So different from "employees."

So different from "personnel."

So different from "human resources."

Talent! Just uttering the word per se makes you puff up and feel good about yourself!

Talent. I do indeed love that word!

"GREEN ROOM" MONSTER?

Whenever I do a TV interview, I always arrive a half-hour early (per producer's instruction), and invariably I am shepherded into a "green room." As often as not, there's a sign over the door that says "TALENT." Just walking under that sign makes me feel about six inches taller!

I love it because of the ... images ... that it brings immediately to mind. Yo-Yo Ma playing the cello. Pavarotti at full volume. Gene Hackman or Nicole Kidman in complete command of a scene. Derek Jeter turning a double play. Michelle Kwan doing a triple axel. Michael Jordan "parting the waters" ... and making that famous last shot that won the Chicago Bulls their sixth championship during his reign with the team.

Oh, and the fabulous guy at, of all places, the international-arrivals hall at Newark airport who sings— yes, *sings*—weary transatlantic travelers toward the baggage-claim area at 6 a.m.

TALENT! *What a word!*

Talent Time: A True Recession-Proof Market

Several years ago, back during the high-roller days of the late 1990s, there was clearly a ... Major Talent Shortage. Guess what? It still exists!

Indeed, it persisted through the recession of 2001– 2002. Yes, unemployment soared. Companies used the downturn as temporary cover while they responded to the permanent White-Collar Revolution. In one guise or another, they had been doing so even before the recession ... and now they had a matchless opportunity to accelerate the process of cutting back on their "human resources" burden.

But companies didn't cut back across the board. Nor did they typically lay off the "last hired." Rather, as several analysts noted, this was the first recession in which seniority did not determine who did or didn't get axed. Instead, layoffs were determined by ... Talent!

Something dramatic was happening. Another development: Usually, a "softening" of the labor market brings with it a leveling-off of productivity. Not this time. In this instance, productivity continued to rock and roll.

Then something else happened that contradicted the historical norm. Even after the economy began to rebound, employment numbers didn't bounce back as quickly or as robustly as they had in the past. Companies were accomplishing more than ever before with the smaller numbers of people who remained—that is, with the ... *Superior Talent* ... that remained. (Hence the productivity gains.) What's more, this "Talent" continued to command hearty financial rewards.

Talent matters to companies more than ever. Which is to say, there *is* a talent shortage. There *will be* a talent shortage for the foreseeable future ... even when there is a "glut" in the "labor market." Because talent is not about "labor." It's not about "head count." It's not about "bodies in the cubicles." Talent is about ... those who score high on the "distinct" scale. And for those with true distinction ... the world will wait in line to acquire their services.

WORSE FOR WAR

Alas, not all company leaders understand that they are fighting a ... War for Talent. I didn't coin that term, but I approve of it. Just as I disapprove of those who think that a change in the business cycle means that they no longer need to fight (yes, fight) for talent.

Ed Michaels, former McKinsey director and coauthor of The War for Talent, *led an exhaustive study of how companies are (or are not) waging this fight. See the Cool Friend interview with Michaels, page 100.*

---

talent

re-imagining the individual

Talent to Date: The Story Thus Far

The Industrial Age is ... over. The white collar paper-processing age is ... over. "Great" products are not enough. (Not nearly enough.) "Great" services are not enough. (Not nearly enough.) You're not going to "make it" in the New Economy solely by pushing TQM (Total Quality Management) or CI (Continuous Improvement) or any of those other New Nostrums that we embraced so vigorously 20 or 30 years ago. New bases for value-added are required—posthaste.

And those new sources of value-added are (all) about ... Creativity! ... Imagination! ... Intellectual Capital! And that stuff is all about ... Talent.

Fundamental premise: We have entered an Age of Talent. "Okay, fine," I can hear you saying. "Put people first. Been there, done that."

No! No! No!

My point is not that "people are cool," or "people are important." It is that … "people" (their talent, their creativity, their intellectual capital, their entrepreneurial drive) is … all the hell there is.

Alas, the language of "talent" has traditionally been limited to a few rarefied realms. Talk opera. Talk symphony. Talk movies. Talk sports. Talk Stanford's physics department. And the talk inevitably turns to … this baritone or that soprano, this cellist or that violinist, this actress or that director, this first baseman or that quarterback, this particle physicist or that mathematical physicist. The talk, in other words, turns almost exclusively to … Talent.

But the … Very Same Logic … applies (must apply) to every other industry and enterprise, public as well as private. Think Microsoft. Think Genentech. Think Fidelity. Think the U.S. Army. Yes, and think Joe and Joan's Chevrolet in God-Knows-Where.

Talent Tomorrow: Dilbert Unbound!

Work is changing. Irreversibly. And now … the "worker" (me, you) must change along with the work.

LAY OFF "WORKERS"

First order of business: We must change the words that we use to describe ourselves. Take the word "worker." Take it … and throw it away. (TRASH CAN TIME. DAMN IT.)

We must expunge that word "worker" from our vocabulary!
We are not "workers." We are individuals. We are … Talent!

Every several generations, we undergo a massive upheaval in our work lives. We move off the farm, with its never-ending rituals (cows don't take holidays; take it from a Vermonter), and into the factory. Then we move out of the factory, with its Simon Legree-like supervisor, and into white-collar nouveau prisons called Big City High-rises.

Today, the software robots are taking over the (surprisingly mindless) white-collar jobs of yesteryear. Once again we must find … Entirely New Ways to Add

"WORKE

"LAND" OF THE BRAVE
Stan Davis and Christopher Meyer, writing in their book *futureWEALTH:* "When land was the productive asset, nations battled over it. The same is happening now ... for talented people."

Talent, indeed, has become the productive asset. And the battle for this insufficiently charted "territory" will test the mettle of all organizations, public as well as private. And merely having a couple of intrepid geniuses at the top won't win this battle. We will win this battle ... and the larger war ... only when our talent pool is both ... Deep and Broad. Only when our organizations are chock-a-block with obstreperous people who are determined to bend the rules at every turn ... and to invent something exciting ... before the other guy does.

SCARY AS HELL

Value. Yet this time around, the change isn't just a matter of moving by the millions like sheep from Job Slot A in the factory to Job Slot B in the high-rise.

"White-collar cubicle slavery," circa 1980, was not all that different from "blue-collar shop-floor slavery," circa 1920. Less heavy lifting, sure, but the Conformity Quotient was about the same: "It's 9 a.m., park your uniqueness at the door, please." But the next shift, the one that is accelerating now, promises to be far more dramatic. Everything even vaguely repetitive will soon be automated. Our only recourse: moving beyond any activity that is even remotely "rote," and moving up—WAY UP!—the New Creativity Scale. Along the way, banishing the Conformity Mandate for good.

We must become ... Independent Contractors ... at least in spirit, if not immediately in reality. We must exhibit ... True Distinction. We must convert ourselves into Genuine Businesspeople ... not mere white-collar ciphers. New me/you: Innovative, Risk-taking, Self-sufficient Entrepreneurs—not smooth-functioning organization men (or women).

Sounds scary as hell, right? You bet.

But here's what I believe ... and I won't mince words. I believe that *Dilbert*-style "cubicle slavery" stinks. I believe that the change now under way is ... Cool. I believe that the chance to tear down those wretched cubicle walls, to take a pickax to that ergonomically

---

DEUTSCH (RE)MARK
German Chancellor Gerhard Schroeder: "Either we modernize or we will be modernized by the unremitting forces of the market."

CHINA SYNDROME
Globalization joins automation in a powerful one-two punch against *Dilbert*-ville. Tom Friedman, writing in a June 2004 column in the *New York Times:* "When I was growing up, my parents used to say to me: 'Finish your dinner—people in China are starving.' I, by contrast, find myself wanting to say to my daughters: 'Finish your homework—people in China and India are starving for your job.' "

We must exhibit …
True Distinction.

correct but numbingly insipid "cubicle furniture," and to make work for ourselves in the wide-open world beyond ... is nothing short of ... Liberation.

What a challenge! What an opportunity! An opportunity for immense, meaningful value creation! An opportunity for individual reinvention!

Millennial Madness

Could it be that the changing world of work is the biggest deal in ... say ... a ... MILLENNIUM? That's more or less the stunning conclusion of a sober Princeton historian-economist. Philip Bobbitt, author of *The Shield of Achilles: War, Peace, and the Course of History*, calls this one of just a half-dozen turning points in human history.

Nations for the last several hundred years have treated their territory as a closed system. And thence the goal was to make the lives of their citizens better, within the confines (key word) of that territory. Well, that goal is no longer tenable, says Bobbitt. The Global Economy is ... well ... erasing that possibility.

Bobbitt claims that the mantle of authority-governance is shifting from the mostly autonomous "nation state" to the globally dependent "market state."

Big idea: If I, as President or Prime Minister, can no longer ensure your welfare within our nation state ... then what's left for me to do is to provide you with tools to survive (and, I hope, thrive) in a truly borderless marketplace for skilled providers of services.

Bobbitt summarizes brilliantly, even if it does make your hair curl: "What strategic motto will dominate this

talent

re-imagining the individual

UNBALANCING ACT
The New (Global) Economy will throw many of our most cherished notions off-kilter. Example: work-life balance.

Keith Hammonds, writing an October 2004 *Fast Company* article called "Balance Is Bunk!":

"The global economy is antibalance. For as much as Accenture and Google say they value an environment that allows workers balance, they're increasingly competing against companies that don't. You're competing against workers with a

lot more to gain than you, who will work harder for less money to get the job done. This is the dark side of the 'happy workaholic' Someday, all of us will have to become workaholics, happy or not, just to get by."

transition from nation-state to market-state? If the slogan that animated the liberal, parliamentary nation-state was 'make the world safe for democracy' ... what will the forthcoming motto be? Perhaps 'making the world available,' which is to say creating new worlds of choice and protecting the autonomy of persons to choose."

President Bill Clinton, who Bobbitt argues understood the coming tectonic economic shift (along with British Prime Minister Tony Blair), echoed Bobbitt's conception: "In a global economy, the government cannot give anybody a guaranteed success story, but you can give people the tools to make the most of their own lives."

BOTTOM LINE:

1. NO NATION IS AN ISLAND.
2. DARWIN RULES! (DISTINCT ... OR EXTINCT.)
3. NO GUARANTEES!
4. HENCE THE ONLY QUASI-GUARANTEES ARE ... GREAT TOOLS WITH WHICH TO COMPETE IN THE (TRUE) GLOBAL VILLAGE.

BOTTOM (BOTTOM) LINE:

1. TERRIFYING.
2. EXHILARATING.
3. COMPLETELY DIFFERENT.

talent

re-imagining the individual

"FREE AGENT" NOTION

For a precise and dramatic rendition of the shifting nature of "employment," you'll do no better than to read Dan Pink's masterful book *Free Agent Nation*. Here are some cold, compelling facts from his file (current as of April 2001):

"Fewer than **1 in 10** Americans now works for a Fortune 500 company."

The **No. 1** private employer in the United States, by body count, is no longer GM or AT&T. It's Manpower, Inc., the temporary work mega-agency.

Between **16 and 25** million
Americans are freelancers or
independent contractors.
There are now
3 million temps—
including temp
lawyers, temp
engineers, temp
project managers,
and even temp CEOs.

3m *TEMPS*

talent

re-imagining the individual

**Microbusinesses, defined as
companies that employ four
or fewer people, are home
to another 12 million to 27
million Americans.**

*In total, then, between 31 million and 55 million Americans are
already occupying "nontraditional" job slots. Job slots whose very
nature would surprise—indeed, horrify—members of our fathers'
generation. (Certainly, they'd knock my father for a loop!)*

IN THE PINK
*Dan Pink has lots more
to say about Free Agent
Nation. All of it incisive
and on point. Read his
book. Or, at least, read
excerpts from the Cool
Friend Interview with him,
page 50.*

Lessons to draw from all this:
1. Lifetime employment is over.
*2. Stable employment at large
corporations is gone.*
*3. The average career will likely
encompass two or three "occupations"
and a half-dozen or more employers.*
*4. Most of us will spend sustained
periods of our career in some form of
self-employment.*
5. Bottom line: We're on our own, folks.

Broken Premise: The Anxiety of Age

Again: The changes afoot in the world of employment are … scary as hell. Especially if you're a 47-year-old accountant, and you've worked in the same white-collar office tower ever since you collected your college diploma 25 summers ago.

Something fundamental is going on—beyond the Tidal Wave of Technology, beyond the Great Job Shift. The nature of "who we are" is undergoing a tectonic shift. The transformation affects not just the kind of work we do, but our fundamental relationship to work. And 47-year-old accountants, watching as reengineering and advanced software automation roar into their cubes, are quaking in their loafers: "What the hell am I going to do … when IBM decides to toss me out of my cubicle?"

They are panicked. And rightfully so.

When I discuss the White-Collar Revolution in my seminars, people respond in one of two very distinct ways. And the breakdown generally runs along what I call the Age 38.5 Divide. If you're less than 38.5 years of age, chances are that you can't wait for dawn to break. If you're more than 38.5 years of age, you're apt to feel seasick … and on the wrong side of a series of broken promises about career certainty.

I don't have any easy answers for those who, chronologically or mentally, find themselves on the wrong side of that Great Divide. Managing our "emigration" to Free Agent Nation won't be easy. It isn't easy.

But we will get it right! And it will be liberating!

SPECIAL WAY

Writing in *Wired* magazine, Michael Goldhaber issued this seminal tough-love statement: "If there is nothing very special about your work, no matter how hard you apply yourself you won't get noticed, and that increasingly means you won't get paid much either."

Cold, hard truth: *Be special—or be spurned.*

They are panicked. And rightfully so.

The key ... and there is only one ... is *attitude*. If the security of guaranteed cubicle slavery for life is your cup of tea ... well, you're going to be scared shitless of all that's coming down the pike. But if the notion of life as a series of "gigs," in which you learn new tricks and live by your wits, excites you ... well, you'll wake up drooling at the chance to re-imagine yourself ... and add yet another memorable-braggable WOW Project to your portfolio.

Can you do it?
Of course!

The United States of ... Att-i-tude

The fact is, the impetus to "reinvent the individual" is nothing new. It is, in fact, quintessentially American. America has historically been a nation that is absolutely defined by self-reinvention.

People didn't like the way things were in Britain, or Germany, or Russia, or Italy, or wherever. So they made a barely imaginable leap of faith (exactly the right term), uprooted themselves, and sailed on unspeakably unpleasant ships for the United States. They landed at an anthill called Ellis Island, or some such. They scrambled, with great difficulty, to find something to do in New York, or some other great city of the East. Then they moved on. A little bit west. A little further west. And so on.

My paternal grandfather left Germany for the United States in the 1870s. My father stayed put, living and working near Baltimore, where Granddad Peters had landed. And so I was raised in Maryland. But then, courtesy of the U.S. Navy, I winged my way to California in 1966. And there I stayed for 35 years.

TRANSCENDENTAL TALENT!
With his concept of "self-reliance," Ralph Waldo Emerson caught the sweet spot of the Brand You attitude. And in his book *Emerson*, Lawrence Buell catches the ... brave essence ... of what Emerson had in mind: "Self-Reliance never comes 'naturally' to adults because they have been so conditioned to think non-authentically that it feels wrenching to do otherwise.

... Self-Reliance [is] a last resort to which a person is driven in desperation only when he or she realizes 'that imitation is suicide; that he must take himself for better, for worse, as his portion.' "

The goal ... for my grandfather, for me, for so many others who followed the call of the frontier ... was always the same: to trade in an old identity for a new one. (I was very proud of the persona called ... California Tom. And quite willing to bury Maryland Tom back in Maryland.)

The Pilgrim Fathers understood this point.

Ben Franklin understood it.

Ralph Waldo Emerson understood it.

Dale Carnegie understood it.

And today Stephen Covey, Tony Robbins, and many, many others understand it.

That is, they understand ... the American Genius for Reinvention. A "genius" that Americans (and, these days, not only Americans) must and will rediscover.

Imagine great-great-grandfather, scrapping along with great-great-grandmother to sustain a tiny farm on the Kansas prairie. They weren't "workers." They weren't "employees." They were, in effect, entrepreneurs ... citizens of an earlier Free Agent Nation.

The good news, then: This is, in fact, a "back to the future" epoch. Our "new world" of WOW Projects and Independent Contracting harkens back to a former "new world" of striking out for the frontier and staking an independent claim.

To say all this about our long and deep heritage of "reinvention" is not to suggest that the current task is easy or painless. Uprooting never was easy. And never will be. But we have done it before ... by the millions ... and will do it again.

YANKEE, COME HOME!

Paul Roberts gets it. Paul has been the prime contractor for the many big projects we've undertaken on our farm in Tinmouth, Vermont. He certainly doesn't talk "management theory." No yapping about "new employment paradigms" from him. But he does the Free Agent Nation walk perfectly. Instinctively, in fact. He lives off his incredible reputation—and yet he knows that he is only as good as his last gig.

A few years back, while preparing to do a TV interview, I was thinking about that Great Age 38.5 Divide. Suddenly, it dawned on me that all those 38.5-plus-year-olds who live in mortal terror of the world outside their corporate cubicle are actually in a minority. And, in the grand scheme of things, they always had been.

I thought about all the people who had worked on projects at our farm during the previous summer. A stone mason. An electrician. A plumber. A tiler. A cabinetmaker. A building contractor. A blacksmith. A well driller. A blaster. A sheep shearer. A veterinarian. And probably a dozen more.

Every one of those folks "got it." Got it a lot more thoroughly, and a lot more personally, than the 47-year-old accountant at Kmart or the 39-year-old middle manager at CSX.

Now it's time for cubicle denizens to get it, too. Time to go "back to the future." (Or else.)

Voices from the Frontier

To paraphrase an old saying: Spirit is the mother of reinvention. Here are some quotations that give voice to that spirit. The "westering" spirit. A spirit that is quintessentially American ... but not just American.

READ. PONDER. REREAD ... ALOUD. AND LISTEN.

talent

re-imagining the individual

"No prudent man dared to be too certain of exactly who he was. ... Everyone had to be prepared to become someone else. To be ready for such perilous transmigrations was to become an American."
—the great historian Daniel Boorstin

"I am an American, Chicago born ... and go at things as I have taught myself, free-style, and will make the record in my own way."
—the eponymous hero of *The Adventures of Augie March*, by Saul Bellow

"You are the storyteller of your own life, and you can create your own legend or not."
—novelist Isabel Allende

"The time seems appropriate to rethink the notions of self and identity in this rapidly changing age."
—Tara Lemmey, Electronic Frontier Foundation

THE "I work for a company called ME" STREET JOURNAL.
THE "rise up and flee your cubicle" STREET JOURNAL.
—"Adventures in Capitalism" advertisements for the
Wall Street Journal

"The new organization of society implied by the triumph of individual autonomy and the true equalization of opportunity based upon merit will lead to very great rewards for merit and great individual autonomy. This will leave individuals far more responsible for themselves than they have been accustomed to being during the industrial period. It will also reduce the unearned advantage in living standards that has been enjoyed by residents of advanced industrial societies throughout the 20th century."
—James Davidson and William Rees-Mogg,
in *The Sovereign Individual*

"BLAME NO ONE! EXPECT NOTHING! DO SOMETHING!"
—sign posted in the New York Jets locker room by then-coach Bill Parcells

"Brand You" ... or Bust

In terms of enterprise—that is, work and business—the upshot of "re-imagining the individual" is a tectonic shift in perspective toward what I call ... Brand You thinking.

I launched this idea as far back as 1997, when I wrote a cover story for *Fast Company* magazine titled "The Brand Called You." Then, in 1999, I authored a book, *The Brand You50*, that explores the idea in considerable depth. That idea, in brief: Whether or not you are on some firm's payroll, you are well advised to behave as if you were CEO of Me Inc. (Translation of the euphemism "well advised": Your professional life—or death—is at stake.)

talent

re-imagining the individual

CEO of Me, Inc.

In other words: View yourself as the boss of your own show, even if that show happens to be playing just now at Citigroup or General Electric or ExxonMobil.

In (still) other words: DISTINCT ... OR EXTINCT.

Branding is a perennially "hot" issue in business circles. Reams and reams of stuff have been written about it, and the emphasis is usually on using "brand image" to sell a product or service. But "branding," at both the individual and the corporate level, is fundamentally not a "marketing" issue. It is an attitude issue, pure and simple. What I call "brand outside" (that is, what the marketplace "experiences of us") is a function of "brand inside" (what lies within us as an enterprise ... or within our individual soul).

In his marvelous book *Corporate Religion*, Danish marketing expert Jesper Kunde writes: "Only with a strong spirit at its foundation can a company achieve a strong market position."

The same goes for you and your career.

(And me and mine.)

HELLO, MR. CHIPS

One group that epitomizes (perhaps surprisingly) the Brand You idea: university professors. People outside academe don't generally realize the degree to which top scholars have become marketing-minded superstars. Yesterday's "absent-minded professor" is today's "entrepreneur of ideas."

Professors' primary loyalty is to their specialty: microbiology, finance, torts. Their primary community encompasses not their putative employer, but their peers in that specialty—all over the globe. They affiliate themselves with a particular institution for some period, mostly based on its offer of research resources, but everything else about them is portable: their labs, their grants, their book contracts, even their pensions.

In fact, their career success depends hardly at all on their "employer," and almost exclusively on that global community of peers—right to the day, for a tiny handful, that they march onto the Swedish stage to accept a Nobel Prize.

DISTINCT
OR
EXTINCT.

10 Degrees of Attitude:
The "Brand You" Survival Kit

If you're going to light out for the frontier … if you're going to reinvent yourself as a Brand You enterprise … then you'll need to pack some key traits in your old kit bag. (I say "if," but it isn't really an option. Remember: Distinct … or Extinct.)

Here are 10 such traits:

1 *Think Like an Entrepreneur.* The point of Brand You is not that you should quit your job at, say, JCPenney. It is that you should re-imagine yourself as the CEO of Me Inc.—who is currently on loan to Penney's for the "next gig." (Perhaps it's a merchandising project for the spring "junior miss" line.) Now, if Penney's keeps serving up Great Gigs, well, maybe you will stick around for 5 or 25 years. But your point of orientation must always be … the degree to which the current Great Gig noticeably enhances your market value.

In sum: Be the de facto boss of your own show. Reinvent all Gigs to ensure that they become Brand You Enhancers.

UPDATE YOUR … ANNUAL REPORT

The rule of thumb is that you should "update your résumé" at least once a year.

I say: Come hell or high water, update your Annual Report *at least once a year. That's what your résumé is, after all—a public announcement that makes the best possible case for your True Commercial Viability and Distinction.*

---

2 *Always Be a "Closer."* If you're going to head up an important enterprise, including one called Me Inc., you obviously need to understand the

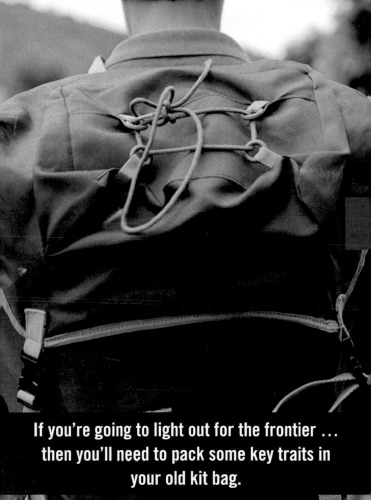

If you're going to light out for the frontier …
then you'll need to pack some key traits in
your old kit bag.

To survive the White-Collar Wipeout …
you need to exhibit … True Mastery.

ins and outs of ... making money. Even if you don't have "line" financial responsibility for your current gig, always make it a point to get acquainted with the numbers ("Follow the money") and keep a close eye on the project P&L and Balance Sheet.

A related point: The track record of Me Inc. derives from only one thing—implemented projects. And implementation is 98 percent a matter of "closing the deal" with a broad array of internal and external stakeholders, many of whom are likely to have conflicting goals. As all true businesspeople know: Life is sales. The rest is details. Or: When it comes to closing the deal, "good try" isn't good enough.

THE "PROVE IT" MOTIVE

In my experience as an employer at a small company, I have all too frequently hired "brilliant people" from giant firms ... who were proverbial ducks out of water when it came to the ABCs of Profit-Making Business.

In Free Agent Nation, that simply won't do. Being able to "show them the money"—or, at least, being able to show "them" that you understand the Basics of Profitable Business—is imperative.

---

3 *Embrace Marketing.* No, you don't need to land a spot on Oprah. But you do need to master much more of the Marketing Puzzle than you probably did in the past. Brand You World is a long way from the old world in which you hung out for 20 years with the same 17 people in the Credit and Collections Department. Instead, you will be going from project to project ... mostly working with strangers. Thus, on each gig, you will be selling yourself anew—marketing your point of view, marketing your worth, marketing Me Inc.

4 *Pursue Mastery.* Competence (and then some) in baseline business skills like marketing and networking is essential. But it's not enough. To survive the White-Collar Wipeout, you need to be Very Damn Special at something of specific economic value. In a word, you need to exhibit ... True Mastery.

Survival merely as Jack R. Smith, Badge 248,

talent

re-imagining the individual

Purchasing Department, is no longer tenable. When I consider Jack for a gig or a full-blown job, I want to see as much distinction—in Jack World terms—as I would if I were considering a trade for a left-handed, fadeaway-throwing set-up man to go into the Boston Red Sox bullpen. In Jack's case, the equivalent of that impossible-to-hit screwball means being best-in-industry at, say, Latin American trade-accounting processes.

"Mastery" goes beyond just having distinct skill. Think about athletes or actors who have records of sustained excellence. These folks are consummate pros who work obsessively at their craft. You should approach your tradecraft in the same way.

> **INTERNATIONAL MAN OF MASTERY**
> *For a great discussion of the "tradecraft" ethos, pick up George Leonard's slender gem of a book on that topic. The title (what else?):* Mastery.

5 *Thrive on Ambiguity.* Mastery is great. Mastery is essential. Yet in a world where the very categories of thought and action are constantly slipping and sliding, even mastery will not suffice. Just as important as the ability to do one thing extremely well is the ability to do a dozen things at once, and change course without raising a bead of sweat or feeling a shred of remorse.

Remember: All bets are off. Everything is up for grabs. Nobody knows what the hell he or she is doing. In such unsettling circumstances, you must be able to not just "deal with," but actually thrive on ambiguity.

6 *Laugh Off Vigorous Screw-ups.* The sweet spot of a Brand You attitude is … a great sense of humor. By sense of humor, I don't mean having a knack for telling off-color after-dinner jokes. No, I mean the ability to laugh off the fabulous prototype that self-destructs … and immediately get on with the next rendition. Reaching and stretching and trying damn near anything is a requisite for survival—let alone some yet-to-be-specified form of New Excellence.

MISTRESS OF IMPROVISATION

Juggling a dozen balls at once is a cinch for most women—and a genetic impossibility for most men. The ability to bob and weave through an uncertain world comes naturally to women. That's one reason (one of many!) why I believe women will be the Masters ... er, Mistresses ... of the New Universe.

talent

re-imagining the individual

In the current Disruptive Age, we will—by definition—be screwing up far more frequently and far more embarrassingly than ever before. Enterprises that tolerate or even celebrate failure ... that encourage the bold bid for greatness that fizzles or goes down in flames ... are the only ones that will succeed.

The same goes for you and me. With or without corporate sanction, we, for survival's sake, must always be playing the Re-imagine Game ... which guarantees black eyes aplenty. Remember, this is not your boss's world (he's probably on the next layoff list anyway); this is your world, your future, your responsibility.

PAINTING ACTION

Can you imagine seeing these signs plastered in Jackson Pollock's workshop?

"Do It Right the First Time!"

"Zero Defects or Bust!"

"Spilled Paint is Wasted Paint!"

"Plan the Work, Work the Plan!"

I think ... not.

---

7 *Relish Technology.* The brutal truth is that lots of people are simply "past their prime" when it comes to "getting" new technologies. (Talk about self-revelation!) But there's hope: You don't need to be a Certificate-bearing Expert in any particular software package; you don't need to be able to program the stuff yourself. But you must ... instinctively appreciate ... the unequivocal fact that the Internet and everything that comes in its wake will turn business upside-down in

---

"WIN" SAM, "LOSE" SAM

Wal*Mart founder Sam Walton had an "absolute fearlessness when it comes to failure." That's what then-CEO of Wal*Mart David Glass told me when I asked him, about a decade ago, to sum up the genius of Sam Moore Walton. Sam was still alive then, and I was making preparations to introduce him at a black-tie shindig at the Waldorf Astoria in New York.

Here's more of what Glass told me:

"Sam will make a sorry mess of something, come in to work the next morning with a chuckle, and comment, 'Well, we got that dumb idea out of the way. What's next?' It's not that he tolerates sloppiness or slackards. To the contrary, it's just that he is a champion of the 'brilliant try,' executed right now, with unparalleled vigor. And if it flops, try something else. Now. With even more vigor. Don't waste even a minute tut-tuting about what might have been."

an astonishingly short period. If that prospect doesn't turn you on … if it doesn't make you tingle with joy and anticipation … well, you're going to be in for a very rough ride. And, I suspect, a very short ride.

HIRE FOR "NET-ITUDE"

It still happens, even today: I run into an executive whose attitude seems to be, "Why the hell did this Internet thing have to happen on my watch?" For shame.

Much better: "This is cool! I don't fully 'get it.' But I'm damned well going to surround myself with people who do get it. And I'm going to listen to them—and then act fearlessly."

---

8 *Grovel Before the Young.* Those of us who are a bit north, say, of that Age 38.5 Divide can indeed have that "appetite for technology." But will we ever truly "get it"? Not a chance! So we must surround ourselves with young people.

The necessary upshot: Every project team must include at least one youngster—someone well under the age of 38.5 (18.5!?)—who doesn't need to "reinvent" himself, because he was born and bred and genetically certified in the New Economy.

9 *Nurture Your Network.* Despite numerous reports to the contrary, I do not believe that "loyalty is dead." I believe that loyalty is … more important than ever. But the Axis of Loyalty has shifted a full 90 degrees. "Old loyalty" was vertical loyalty. Loyalty to a hierarchy: You grasped one rung after another as you scrambled up a prescribed vertical ladder. Call it "suck-up loyalty," if you will. That's going, going, gone. And good riddance!

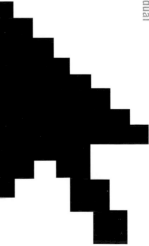

Grovel before the young.

"New loyalty" is horizontal loyalty. Loyalty to a trade or industry: What matters is what your peers think of your work. Which puts a high premium on developing what I call the Rolodex Obsession. You must build—and deliberately manage!—an ever-expanding, ever-deepening network of professional contacts throughout your field.

LIGHTS! CAMERA! ... TALENT!

As others have noted, the project-driven, "new loyalty"-oriented New Economy follows the so-called Hollywood Model, in which one goes from one production "company" to another—seeing a few familiar faces at the start of each outing, but mostly working with new people on new stuff.

In that world, success depends completely on having a good rep among your peers. If you want (say) to be on the lighting crew of the next Oscar-buzz-worthy film, you need people "in the industry" who will say to the chief cinematographer of that project, "If you're going to be doing lots of soft-light shooting, give Joanne Brown a call. I've never seen anyone with chops as good as hers; she's also a pleasure to work with."

---

10 *Cultivate a Passion for Renewal.* Picking up new skills on a catch-as-catch-can, as-needed basis used to be a reasonable career strategy. But these days, a passive approach to professional growth will leave you gathering splinters on the bench, or off the roster entirely. Revolutionizing your Portfolio of Skills ... at least every half-dozen years, if not more often, is now a ... Minimum Survival Necessity.

Query: Do you have a formal R.I.P. (Renewal Investment Plan)? And if you do have one, is it as bold as these bold times demand?

talent

re-imagining the individual

BUILD YOUR BRAIN, BUILD YOUR BRAND

Here, adapted from an outstanding recent book—Dennis Littky's *The Big Picture: Education Is Everyone's Business* (2004)—is another list of traits that you should make room for in your Brand You Survival Kit:

- Be a lifelong learner
- Be passionate
- Be ready to take risks
- Be able to think critically
- Be able to look at things differently
- Be creative
- Be able to persevere
- Have integrity and self-respect
- Have moral courage
- Be able to use the world around you
- Be able to give back to your community
- Be able to work independently and with others
- Speak well, write well, read well, and work well with numbers
- TRULY ENJOY YOUR LIFE AND WORK

A "Brand You" Start

In the Brand You training offered by Tom Peters Company, we provide concrete ways for clients to renew their Brand You portfolio. They have found one exercise in particular to be of value. We call it the Personal Brand Equity Evaluation. Each participant is asked to complete the following statements:

I am known for ...

_____

_____

_____

_____

Next year at this time I will also be known for ...

_____

_____

_____

My current project is challenging me in these ways ...

_____

_____

_____

_____

New things I've learned in the last 90 days include ...

_____

_____

_____

_____

_____

_____

talent

re-imagining the individual

My public "recognition program" consists of ...

_____

_____

_____

Additions to my Rolodex in the last 90 days include ...

_____

_____

_____

_____

My résumé today is Discernibly Different from my résumé last year at this time in these ways ...

_____

_____

_____

_____

_____

There's no magic here. But applying the "brand equity" idea to your career is a clear winner, or so clients keep telling us.

WORD EQUITY

"Personal." "Brand." "Equity."

Yes: You and I are BRANDS. As much as Coca-Cola is a brand. Thus, you and I have a (high or low) (growing or declining) (solid or fragile) brand equity.

Please: Don't just nod your head when you read that.

Please: Take in the full denotation and connotation of that term.

Words are important. They have value. They have (dare I say?) equity.

Talent Means Work

This chapter is ... personal. This book is ... personal. Talent is personal. For me. For you.

The theme of Talent goes to ... the root and branch of Who We Are and What We Do. It gets at ... how we contend with those millenial forces that are tearing away at White-Collar World. The forces that are turning *Dilbert*-style cubicle slavery into not just a joke, but an unsustainable anachronism.

Again, my mantra for life in a Brand You world:
DISTINCT ...
OR EXTINCT!

What makes for True Distincion in this Age of Talent? Truly distinct talent reveals itself through ... Work. Through weird, wild projects that add Incomparable Value and effect Profound Transformation.

The remaining chapters in this book will show you how to distinguish yourself as Talent by adding WOW Projects to your "portfolio," the Sales25 to your skill set, and Weird Thinking to your repertoire.

THE "SALLY" ADVANTAGE

My colleague Sally Helgesen provides a list of key attitudinal attributes in her book *Thriving in 24/7*. She and I arrived at our ideas separately, but not surprisingly her approach to "24/7 World" matches my approach to "Brand You World":

Start at the core. Take regular inventory of where you are. To remain nimble, locate your "inner voice."

Learn to zigzag. Think "gigs." Think life-long learning. Forget "old loyalty." Work on optimism.

Create your own work. Articulate your value. Integrate your passions.

Identify your market. Run your own business.

Weave a strong web of inclusion. Build your own support network. Master the essential art of "looking people up."

TOP 10 TO-DOs

1. *Lose your "job" ... mentality.* Wean yourself from usage of the words "worker," "employee," and "job." For the latter, think *gig*. Think *project*. And in general, think *Talent, Talent, Talent!*

2. *Jump on it.* So you are perched on a cliff known as "lifetime employment." Get over it! Jump off of it! Learn to bungee-jump!

3. *Wish upon a star.* Which star? *You*—you're the star ... and don't forget it. Hence, the Hollywood model of Talent applies. See yourself as a *hot property* who deals in *bankable projects*.

4. *Hire someone you know.* Namely, *yourself*. Assume that no one else will hire you ... not because you aren't Grade-A Talent, but because "CEO of Me, Inc." is the only position that you can count on.

5. *Beg to differ.* Branding (for a company, for *you*) is about difference ... *dramatic difference*. How are you *unique?* Figure it out. Play it up. Make it count.

6. *Be an "equity" investor.* At least once a year, do the Personal Brand Equity Evaluation that I describe above (page 46). You are a brand. Brands have equity. So keep close tabs on *your* equity.

7. *Rave on.* Pick a recent project of yours, and write a review of your work on it as if the project were a movie ... and you were an actor or director. (Go ahead: Give yourself four stars!)

8. *Make your mark.* Hire a professional Designer to create a logo for Brand You. A logo will help you sell yourself ... and the process of designing it will you help you *define* yourself.

9. *Analyze this.* Draft a report on "Me, Inc." as if you were a securities analyst for a major (Talent!) brokerage firm.

10. *Don't look back.* Lighting out for the Brave New Frontier of Brand You World is ... Not Optional. So remember: *Distinct—or Extinct.*

COOL FRIEND: Daniel Pink

Dan Pink is the author, most recently, of **A Whole New Mind** *(Riverhead, March 2005). He is a contributing editor at* **Wired** *magazine, and he has also written for the* **New York Times, Harvard Business Review,** *and* **Fast Company.** *Formerly a speechwriter for Vice President Al Gore, he now lives the free-agent life in Washington, D.C. Below are remarks that he made in connection with his first book,* **Free Agent Nation: The Future of Working for Yourself** *(2001).*

* *

[W]e used to have a system in this country where companies offered employees security, and employees offered companies loyalty. That bargain has come undone. Anybody who still believes it is a fool.

* *

Paternalism in corporate America was something that was not only prominent, it was in many ways explicit. So the phone company where my grandfather worked was known as "Ma Bell." Kodak in Rochester, New York, was known as "The great yellow father." Metropolitan Life Insurance was known as "Mother Met." There was this notion that companies would operate like parents, and they would take care of their employees like they took care of children. And that came undone in the late 1980s and early 1990s.

And for a lot of American workers, it was like the end of adolescence. They no longer were going to be taken care of, and they had the simultaneously exhilarating and terrifying feeling of being forced to navigate their own way. So the end of economic adolescence is one reason for the beginning of free agency.

* *

Free agency is essentially Karl Marx's revenge, because workers can now own the means of production. In the industrial economy, the tools you needed to create wealth were large, expensive, and difficult for one person to operate. But now the tools—such as a laptop—are small, affordable, and easy for one person to operate.

I have a modest home office. I've got two computers in this office—more computing power than was on Apollo 11. And the tools of the means of production are easy for one person to operate.

* *

[T]he nature of corporations has changed. For instance, we used to expect corporations to be around forever. But that's not true anymore. Think about Netscape. Netscape, which was a success, a huge success, was founded in '94, went public in '95, then essentially disappeared in early 1999. It had a life span of just over four years. So, was Netscape a company or was Netscape just a really cool project?

And then you ask yourself, does it even matter? Because what did Netscape do? It put a good product on the market, it challenged a big company, it equipped lots of people with new skills and connections, it made some people wealthy.

* *

[T]he life span of every company is shrinking. And this is happening at the same time that the life span of individuals is increasing. Basically, any individual can expect to outlive any organization for which he or she works. So let me raise a Zen-like metaphysical question: how do you have lifetime job security when you're going to outlive the organization?

Think about how much of your mortgage money you would bet on whether Amazon.com will be here in 10 years, or whether even General Motors will be here in 10 years, or any other company. In my grandfather's day if I had said to him, "Do you think the phone company, Ma Bell, will be here in 10 years?" he would have said, "Of course."

* *

I think in general free agency is a great thing. To my mind, the glass is three-quarters full.

* *

[T]here is tremendous loyalty in the work force today. Yet it's a very different kind of loyalty from the Eisenhower era. ... You know, that was what I would call vertical loyalty. It ran up and down, from the individual to the organization. And what I think is happening right now is a more horizontal loyalty.

It's loyalty to teams, it's loyalty to projects, it's loyalty to products, it's loyalty to colleagues, it's loyalty to ex-colleagues, it's loyalty to professions, it's loyalty to family. Instead of a single up or down node, you have multiple horizontal connections. And to my mind, that's actually a more robust form of loyalty.

* *

The underlying operating system of the free agent economy ... is really nothing more than the Golden Rule; it's reciprocal altruism. "You're good to me—I'm good to you." And, you know, reciprocal altruism is an aspect of many species, including ours, and reciprocal altruism, the Golden Rule, also happens to be the cornerstone of every major world religion.

* *

When your clone and my clone 200 years from now are looking back at the regime of what we consider traditional employment—full-time, year-round work in the service of a large organization, the predominant form of work in the last half of the 20th century—they're going to say, "Ooh, wait a second, that was a very strange aberration."

Yet today we think that that form of employment is the right and proper and natural form of employment, and that any deviation from it is some strange, exotic beast. ... [But] I actually think that the regime of big government, big labor, big corporations squashed a lot of these more fundamental human instincts like the Golden Rule.

* *

Traditional jobs are beginning to resemble free agent
employment. Job tenure is shrinking. People go into
a job saying, "I'll stick around for a year or two." The
border between who's a free agent and who's a traditional
employee is going to be harder to detect, and it's going to
matter even less.

Also, it's not as if you have to pick a side, and
then stay there forever. ... More and more people will
be holding dual passports in Free Agent Nation and in
Corporate America. They'll be doing time in Corporate
America, they'll be coming to Free Agent Nation, they'll
be going back, and so forth.

* *

[W]e're on the brink of a feminine century. The border
between what is work and what is home is blurring,
becoming ambiguous. The border between what is work
and what is play is blurring. It's becoming ambiguous.
The borderline between what's a company and what's a
project is growing muddier. The borderline between who's
an employee and who's a free agent is growing murkier.
Women, in general, are much better at dealing with
ambiguity than men are.

Given the way this economy operates, women are
going to have a comparative advantage, in that men are
going to have to start acting much more like women. Now
fortunately for me, I live in a house with three women, or
two girls and a woman.

* *

I have this notion of the new office that will be
what I call the Free Agent Elk's Lodge. In the Adams-
Morgan area of Washington, D.C., somebody has
opened something called "The Affinity Lab." Essentially
they're renting out desks and common areas to small
entrepreneurs and free agents. It's not really an executive
suite, and it's not really an incubator. I'm not sure what
it is, but it's pretty cool. It's a free-agent Elk's Lodge.
So here it is, off the pages of my book, into the heart of
Adams-Morgan.

2

Making Work Matter:
The WOW Project!

Contrasts

Was	Is
A job	A performance
Puttin' in time	Puttin' on the Ritz
"Phoning it in"	Fully "in the moment"
Forgettable	Memorable
A bureaucratic task	A signature piece
Faceless	Full of "character"
A descent into routine	A plunge into the unknown
Largely invisible	Immediately transparent
Another day's work	A product of enormous investment
"Acceptable work"	Mastery of craft
Numbing	Exhausting
Enervated employees	Energized performers
Tepid	Hot
Pastel	Technicolor
Predictable (It's "ho-hum")	Quirky ("It matters!")
Risk-averse	Adventuresome
Hunkering down	Reaching Out
"Another day older"	"A growth experience"
"Colors within the lines"	"Curious to a fault"
Boss-driven (Suck-up City)	Project-driven (Teamwork City)

!Rant

We are not prepared ...

We too often view ourselves as **victims of heartless organizations**, as pawns, as **hapless and helpless "cubicle slaves"** • **WE MUST REMIND OURSELVES THAT THE WHITE-COLLAR REVOLUTION WILL ERASE ALL OF THAT. WE MUST UNDERSTAND THAT IN THE NEW ECONOMY ALL WORK IS PROJECT WORK—AND THAT EVERY PROJECT MUST BE A *WOW* PROJECT.** • (Or else.) • ("Or else" means "No role whatsoever" ... for **cubicle slaves** content to perform "rote chores.")

!Vision

I imagine ...

A world where ... **WORK MATTERS.**

A world where ... *Dilbert* Is Denied.

A world where ... **WE LEARN SOMETHING NEW EVERY DAY**.

A world where ... we revel in the thrill of changing times.

A world where ... **WE CAN *BRAG* ABOUT WHAT WE DO**. ("Brag" = Big Word.)

WOW—What Is It Good For?

In *The Leader's Voice*, my colleagues Boyd Clarke and Ron Crossland tell a wonderful story about Marilyn Carlson Nelson. When Marilyn was a girl, she told her dad, Kurt Carlson (owner of the Carlson Travel network), that she thought Sunday School was dull. She felt the time had come for her to start going to adult church.

Young Miss C. got an earful from Dear Old Dad. He said it was not time to go to adult church. Instead, he told her: "If you don't like Sunday School, change it."

So she did.

That was ... for all intents and purposes ... Marilyn Carlson's First WOW Project. But hardly her last. She's now Big Boss of the entire Carlson mega-enterprise.

Marilyn Carlson learned early on that the road to success was paved with ... WOW Projects.

Project: a task that has a beginning and an end, as well as deliverables along the way.

WOW Project: one that has "goals and objectives" that inspire. And inspire others.

talent

!

the WOW project!

WOW Projects are ...

- Projects that Matter.
- Projects that Make a Difference.
- Projects that you can Brag About ... forever.
- Projects that Transform the Enterprise.
- Projects that Take Your Breath Away.
- Projects that make you/me/us/"them" Smile.
- Projects that Highlight the Value that You Add ... and Why ... You Are Here on Earth. (Yes. That Big.)

WOW Projects are ... not hype.

WOW Projects are ... an Absolute Necessity.

THIS OLD WHITE GUY CAN *JUMP*

There's not much that I dislike more in Seminar World than "motivational gurus" who devote every other slide in their presentation to some pithy quote from an Old White Guy, dead 500 years. Still, every now and then, one of those Old White Guys got it right. And nobody got it more right than Michelangelo when he said: "The greatest danger for most of us is not that our aim is too high and we miss it, but that it is too low and we reach it."

Yes!

Projects that Highlight the Value that You Add ... and Why ... You are Here on Earth.

(Yes. That Big.)

The Tao of WOW

The best way to get at the Quintessential Spirit of the WOW Project is to listen to those who "get it."

First up ... Roseanne! "Nobody gives you power," she said. "You just take it."

"Obeying the rules," writes Harriet Rubin in *The Princessa: Machiavelli for Women*, "is obeying their rules. [Women] can never be powerful as long as they try to be in charge the same way men take charge."

Henry Louis Gates Jr. put it this way in a commencement address at Hamilton College: "Don't just express yourself. Invent yourself. And don't restrict yourself to off-the-shelf models."

The great ballet choreographer Sergei Diaghilev routinely begged his prima ballerinas: "Astonish me!"

Former president of Nintendo Hiroshi Yamauchi, when the company's top game designer asked him what to do next, said: "Build something great!"

Legendary ad man David Ogilvy asked by a copywriter about the desired outcome of a project, said (in essence):

Make it
immortal!

WRITE WHEN YOU FIND "WORK"

There's a funny thing about management books. They talk about "organization structure." About "motivation." About "marketing strategies."

They talk about damn near everything. Except for ... THE WORK ITSELF.

I don't give two hoots in hell about "structure" or "strategy." I like "doing stuff." That is, I am obsessed about ... THE WORK ITSELF. Work that ... Matters. Work you can ... Brag About.

My mantra: It's WOW Projects, stupid.

The "How" of WOW

How should you evaluate a project? Any project? Every project? My answer is simple: Is it ... WOW? Does it ... "take your breath away"?

"ASTONISH ME."

"Take your breath away." In these ... yes ... Breathtaking Times ... shouldn't that be the Goal of Anything that You Do? Isn't that routinely what a ballplayer tries to do during a ball game? Isn't that routinely what a cellist tries to do during a three-minute solo? Why the hell shouldn't that be what you try to do ... in ... Finance ... Engineering ... Human Resources ... Information Systems?

In my book *The Project50*, I urge readers to measure every project that they undertake along four dimensions (and to measure each dimension quantitatively):

WOW!
BEAUTY!
IMPACT!
RAVING FANS!

talent

!

the WOW project!

RAVING REVIEW

I stole that last "dimension" from Ken Blanchard and Sheldon Bowles, who in their book Raving Fans *tell readers to ask themselves: Do customers "rave" about what we do?*

Rave!

Not: "Are you 'satisfied'?"

Not: "Did we 'exceed expectations'?"

Rave = Very Cool Word.

Rave = Very Big Word.

(Not so incidentally, Mr. Bowles invented this idea while running a string of discount gas stations in the Canadian wilds. Not an arena for "raving fans," you'd think. Think again! No limits.)

So what, in particular, do I mean when I refer to measuring the "WOW" dimension? Consider your current project, or your portfolio of departmental projects if you're the chief. On a scale of 1 to 10, rate each project more or less as follows:

1.
"Another day's work. Pays the rent."

4.
"We do something 'of value.' "

7.
"Pretty damn cool (and definitely subversive)."

10.
"WE AIM TO CHANGE THE WORLD."

Legacy: Leaving WOW in Your Wake

Legacy. L-e-g-a-c-y. It's a Huge word. It asks, "Did I Matter?" (Yikes.)

Legacy is not a word that applies only to those who are over age 60. It is a word for all of us ... all the time.

A few years ago, I had a dispiriting session in Bermuda with several of that country's top CEOs. The meeting took place not long after the imposition of the new, restrictive Sarbanes-Oxley financial-services legislation, and they said they felt trapped.

I wasn't very helpful. I said, "Baloney."

I continued: "You are ... C-E-Os. By mortal standards, that's a ... Big Deal. So the issue—THE ISSUE—is whether you see these new 'restraints' as 'restraining' or disguised 'opportunities.' "

I was so frustrated by the undercurrent of negativism that I finally said (to these Very Powerful People): "Please leap forward to 2007, then 2012. Write a Brief Business History of Bermuda. WHAT WILL HAVE BEEN SAID ABOUT ... YOUR COMPANY ... DURING YOUR TENURE AT THE TOP?

"Somehow," I added with perhaps a sniff of sarcasm, "I doubt you'll write, 'I was flummoxed by regulation and really didn't get much done.' "

Distressed by what I'd seen and heard at this "CEO Summit," I was very happy the next morning to move on to a meeting with ... Kids!

talent

!

the WOW project!

BHAG MAN

Jim Collins, co-author of *Built to Last* and author of *Good to Great*, and I disagree about a lot of things. But one idea of his that I LOVE ... is the dire necessity for every project to have a ... BHAG.

BHAG: Big Hairy Audacious Goal.

Awesome term. Awesome ... indeed, audacious ... concept.

BETTER WOW THAN "WELL"

For me, WOW is personal. If I don't aim for WOW, then I just feel that ... I might as well not aim at all. An October 2003 piece on my book *Re-imagine!* in *Fast Company* "got me" to a T: "In Tom's World, it's always better to try a swan dive and deliver a colossal belly flop than to step timidly off the board while holding your nose." Yes!

A year later, in a fall 2004 radio interview, I inadvertently "got" myself—and (I humbly believe) summarized the spirit of WOW. "I'd rather be 'interesting' than 'right,' " I said.

Again: Yes!

Reward
EXCELLENT
Failures!

Punish
MEDIOCRE
Successes.

At a formal session with "Future Leaders of Bermuda" I was ... bombarded by the ... Toughest Questions ... I've ever faced:

"What's your vision of the future?"

"Do you feel that you have an obligation to make the world better?"

"What have you accomplished since your first book 20 years ago?"

WOW! Talk about stretching!

Why! Why! Why ... aren't questions from 50-year-olds as ... Fundamental ... as those from 20-year-olds?

Why?

Nothing Succeeds Like ... Failure

Phil Daniels is a successful Australian businessman who attended a seminar I gave in Sydney. Amid an audience of over 1,000 people, he stood up to support a point I'd made. But what he said ended up making me see the world in a different light. His career success, Daniels said, flowed from a "very simple philosophy."

Two sentences. Six words. Namely:

"Reward excellent failures."

"Punish mediocre successes."

I love that!

In my master PowerPoint presentation, I have well over 1,000 slides. By definition, one of them must rank highest on the Provocative/Important scale. In my mind ... The Daniels Formula ... occupies that lofty spot.

An "excellent failure": You take a Bold, Brash, Brassy Leap Forward. Oops ... it doesn't work. And you end up on your hindquarters ... bruised and battered. Good for you! You went for it! You got a heady whiff of the Land of WOW! That whiff, despite the subsequent bruises, eggs you on toward your Gold Medal in information systems or in training.

It's simple (if daunting): No true WOW project ever comes into being without ... a willingness to court ... Excellent Failures.

In a world where ... confusion reigns ... where we must ... Experiment Our Way into the Future ... the Only Way Forward is to ... Court and Reward Excellent Failures. (NO BULL.)

PEAK (AND VALLEY) EXPERIENCES

I spent 30 years living among the "excellent failures" of Silicon Valley. They were a hallmark of Valley Culture, long before Dot-Com Madness came along. Somewhere in Santa Clara County, there is a Business Cemetery of the Mind, where you'll find thousands of unmarked graves of failed computer companies, failed semiconductor companies, failed software companies—and, yes, failed dot-com companies.

Several economists, all of them wiser on this issue than I am, have argued that those Bold Failures are not just a "byproduct" of the Valley's success; they are the Primary Enabler thereof.

talent !
the WOW project!

The JAMS Jam

Now to the flip side of the Daniels Formula ... "Punish mediocre successes."

Problem: "Mediocre successes" may be just fine ... for Mediocre Times. But these are not ... mediocre times. These are not times that demand "a bit of" or "a touch of." These are times that demand ... Going For It.

WOW or Wuss!

Excellent or Extinct!

Different or Dead!

So let's make this our motto for the times:

No damn JAMS! P-E-R-I-O-D!

No more ... "Just Another Mediocre Success."

PRESS "RELEASE!" (PLEASE)

I pick up the *Wall Street Journal*. News flash: A giant company has announced a "major" reorganization. One unit will be hitched to another unit—in order to make doing business somewhat easier. Nothing wrong with that.

The problem: There is nothing *right* about it, either! Here is a company that's going nowhere. It's beset with killer problems. And this announcement fails to address the deep, unspoken issues that keep it from moving forward. Shifting the boxes on the org chart—that's all that I see here. The word "WOW"? I can't imagine anyone at this company ever using such a word.

WOW or Wuss!

MEDIOCRE SUCCESS =

BIG

TROUBLE

Far too many intelligent people waste far too much effort in pursuing ... Just Another Mediocre Success.

I clearly remember when I started airing the Daniels Shtick in my presentations. I was speaking to the top 300 officers of one of our largest financial services companies. The CEO was startlingly silent throughout my remarks, but he approached me afterward.

"You pretty much ruined my day, though I'll pay you for your services," he said with half a laugh, and with more than a little chagrin. "It was that 'mediocre successes' thing. We are dependent upon the quality of our information technology. We launch project after project. Truth told, spend tens of millions of dollars a year. And the simple fact is, after those projects have been dumbed down and politicized by various factions within the enterprise—well, damn it, virtually all of them end up as 'mediocre successes.' I'm beside myself. Maybe there's some intriguing merit in the other half of your friend's idea: 'Reward excellent failures.' I'm going to think on that."

I trust that he did. And that you will, too.

JACK, OUT OF THE BOX (AS USUAL)

Jack Welch once made essentially the same point as Phil Daniels. Welch said that nobody who worked for him ever got in trouble for swinging for the fences and missing. What people got in trouble for was spending two years on a project that—even if it succeeded—wasn't going to make the world wobble on its axis.

That is: Mediocre Success = Big Trouble.

WOW FOR WOW'S SAKE

Hot off the presses (in 2005) comes a book that I have added to my Library of WOW: *The Art of Business: Make All Your Work a Work of Art*, by Stan Davis and David McIntosh.

The authors argue that people must adopt these "four elements" of new business thinking:

"See yourself as an artist."
"See your work as a work of art."
"See your customers as an audience."
"See your competition as teachers."

Larry Summers, economist and current president of Harvard, blurbed the book this way: "The Art of Business is a good antidote to all the business-as-war books."

By the way, Stan Davis, an old pal of mine, was a tough-minded "strategy guy" when I first met him. And now he sees business as *art*, of all things!

All I can say is: Wow!

talent

the WOW project!

The Wasted Life: How Not to WOW

In my seminars, I frequently point to a *Fortune* magazine story that compared the most admired corporations in the world to the "also-rans." The losers had in common a tendency to focus on these four goals (LHMGs: "Little Hairless Mediocre Goals"?):

"Minimize risk."

"Respect the chain of command."

"Support the boss."

"Make budget."

Aargh!

What a (timid) way to live!

But often as not, when I cite that report, people confront me by saying: "Tom, you just don't get the 'real world.'" In the real world, they say, respecting the chain of command is "where it's at" ... supporting the boss is "nonnegotiable" ... making budget is "critical" ... minimizing risk is "essential."

Then I attack. Savagely.

"Look at a damn history book," I spit. "Go and get your 10th-grade daughter's text. Pull out 50 names. Drop the jerks (Hitler, Stalin). Then look at the rest. Jefferson. Washington. Hamilton. Steinem. Madame Curie. Einstein. Newton. Picasso. De Gaulle. Churchill. Gandhi. King.

"Did anyone on that list 'minimize risk'? (I utter that phrase with dripping contempt.) 'Respect the chain of command'? 'Support the boss'? 'Make budget'?"

talent

the WOW project!

THE VOICE OF WOW

Whence comes WOW? From *passion*. And from *passionate people*.

Diane Geppi-Aikens was a gifted lacrosse coach. Her teams outperformed their potential by a country mile—year in and year out. More important, many of her players had their lives transformed permanently by exposure to this extraordinary woman.

In a tribute to Geppi-Aikens after her untimely death, player upon player commented on the lengths to which she would go to instill her abiding passion for passion.

For example (from the 2004 book *Lucky Every Day: The Wisdom of Diane Geppi-Aikens*, by Chip Silverman): "She made us close our eyes and hear the singers she was

passionate about: Roberta Flack and Aretha Franklin. 'Listen to the joy in their voices,' urged Diane. 'It's not the words or the music. They sing with such great passion; such heart and soul. You can feel how the singers love what they are doing. It's not just a job to them. ... If you want to excel, you need to be passionate! Otherwise, why waste your time?' "

What I really want to do is to put those "real world" people to ... The Epitaph Test. I wonder whether any of them, down deep, would want one of these epitaphs:

Joe J. Jones

1942–2005

He always made budget.

(Or: "He minimized risk")
(Or: "He respected the chain of command.")
(Or: "He supported the boss.")

Joe J. Jones

1942–2005

CEO, 1993–2005

He hit quarterly earnings targets 44 times in a row.

Now, there is nothing "wrong" with any of the above. The problem: There is nothing "right" about any of the above, either.

WOW Is Me: The Red Exclamation Mark

For better or for worse, I buy my own act. I shun the ... Mediocre Goals ... of "also-ran" companies. Along with Steve Jobs, I say, "Let's make a dent in the universe." And I believe that the ... Essence of Enterprise Excellence in Disruptive Times ... is ... the ... Relentless Pursuit of WOW.

All of which came to a "point" (you'll see what I mean by "point" in a moment) when I tackled a particular WOW Project of my own. Several years ago, I decided to re-brand my company. To give the Tom Peters Company a new look, a new logo. It was a daunting task. I worked with a designer, Ken Silvia, who is so simpatico with me that we finish each other's sentences.

It took us over a year and a half. And you know what we ended up with as a logo: a red exclamation mark (!).

Yes!

One-point-five years to create ... a "simple" red exclamation mark. And I couldn't have been more ecstatic.

Red Marks the Spot

Before you is a field of red exclamation marks. They represent the various Moods of WOW.

Go ahead. Chuckle. But we think it's as powerful ... though not (yet) as valuable ... as the Nike Swoosh.

What do the last 30-odd years of my professional life add up to? Simple. A RED EXCLAMATION MARK.

Please, do not steal my logo. But please, do steal the Spirit of the Logo.

The Spirit of WOW!

Weekend WOW

Scenes from a trip to New York City ...

Thursday night. The Orchestra of St. Lukes, under Sir Charles Mackerras's inspired direction, performs "A Haydn Miscellany" at Carnegie Hall.

Friday night. The Metropolitan Opera, with Plácido Domingo, presents a stunning Simon Boccanegra.

Saturday morning. At Rizzoli's bookstore, I pick up a copy of *Cities in Civilization*, by Sir Peter Hall.

Somewhere along the way, it occurs to me that the production of each of those "events" was a WOW Project ... and thus a long (long) way from a *Dilbert*-style "dreary day at the office."

The difference is immense. THINK ABOUT IT.

TOP 10 TO-DOs

1. *Get ready for the "gig" time.* Start viewing your career as a necklace strung with pearls ... aka "projects." Definition of "project": a discrete, would-be WOW-worthy effort to get some particular thing *done*. In Brand You world, all work is project work.

2. *Make it matter.* Is work just "what I do." Or is it "who I am and how I make a strong, salient impact on the world"? Oh, please, say that it's the latter. Work That Matters is the only ... Work That Wows.

3. *Take it away.* Take power, that is. No one will give it to you ... but ultimately, no one can keep it from you—if you resolve to take as much as you need in behalf of your WOW Project.

4. *Pass it on.* Every project you do adds to (or subtracts from) the legacy that you leave. Your ultimate project? *Posterity.*

5. *Say no to "so-so."* Give "good enough" a good kick. Punish mediocre successes. (The road to career hell is paved with them.)

6. *Fail your way to success.* Give a big kiss to the magnificent miss. Reward excellent failures. (They pave the way to WOW.)

7. *Put in in the BHAG.* Build your every project around a ... Big Hairy Audacious Goal. Mantra: No BHAG, no WOW.

8. *Recast your résumé.* Open your résumé file, and reorganize every item on it into one of three categories: "Mediocre Success," "Excellent Failure," "WOW." The results will reveal how well you are (or are not) managing your Talent.

9. *Trade coasting for boasting.* Treat each project as a way to earn Bragging Rights. Forget "Take it easy." Instead, "Talk it up!"

10. *Carve it in stone.* Write your ideal epitaph. I mean it: Get out pen and paper, and "etch" the statement that you hope will summarize your work life. Now: Live up to it. Live up to .... WOW!

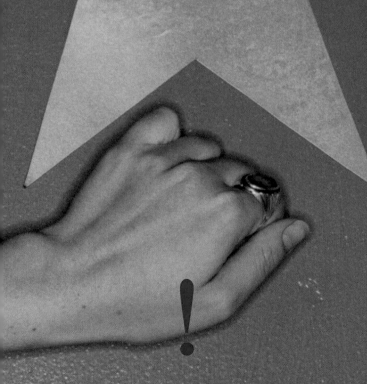

3

No Limits:
WOW Projects for the
"Powerless"

Contrasts

Was	Is
Know your place	Do your thing
Wait	Act
Follow "the rules"	Make new rules
Accept assignments	Remake assignments
Play it as it lays	Make it up as you go
Get along to go along	Get up and go
Constrained by seniority (your lack thereof)	Amused by "seniority" (pretensions thereof)
Barriers	Opportunities
"No power (alas)"	"No constraints (yes!)"
Cubicle slave	Free agent

!Rant

We are not prepared ...

We labor under the delusion that we must **"WAIT OUR TURN"** ... that we must **"WORK OUR WAY UP THE ORGANIZATION LADDER."** • But the decimation of hierarchies, **the deconstruction of career ladders,** and the redefinition of Work-of-Value make that a false— nay, a ***dangerous***—assumption. • So we must **GRASP THE NETTLE AT THE BEGINNING OF EVERY JOB AND EVERY ASSIGNMENT.** • We must appreciate the **power that comes with being** "powerless" ... and **TURN EVERY OSTENSIBLY MUNDANE "TASK" INTO A WOW PROJECT!**

!Vision

I imagine ...

A 24-year-old "independent contributor," working under the auspices of **Enormous Enterprise Inc.** • While she is at EE Inc., **SHE GETS TOTALLY TURNED ON BY ... WI-FI.** • She chats up some Wi-Fi experts. She leverages her growing knowledge—and her boundless enthusiasm—to cadge a few bucks from vendors. **(Perhaps with minimal "chain of command" approval. PERHAPS WITH NO APPROVAL WHATEVER.)** • And she gets a Beachhead Wi-Fi Project going at EE Inc. • Afterward, the world is **never the same again** for the company. (Or for our 24-year-old "independent contributor.")

Autobiography: "Powerless" Like Me

My seminar had gone on for a couple of hours. It was time for the first break. A relatively young man approached me. He was a fairly junior staffer in finance, it turns out. He began with flattery: "This is really great stuff." (I beamed. Naturally.)

"REVEL IN MY POWERLESSNESS"

Then it came—the phrase that mothballed a thousand ships. "But I'm not a vice president," he said. "I can't implement any of this stuff. I don't have the power."

"I don't have the power."

What do I do? I flip out. Okay, not true. My mom taught me to be polite, so I'm polite.

But inside I'm flipping out.

Can you imagine Martin Luther King, Jr., saying, "Civil Rights is Cool, but I don't have the power"? Can you imagine Gandhi saying "The Brits stink, but I don't have the power"? Or Charles de Gaulle in Britain following the fall of France in 1940: isolated, a longtime maverick and outcast within the French Army, recently convicted of treason by a kangaroo court in Petain's France? Can you imagine de Gaulle, at that moment, saying, "FuhgeddabouditIdon'thavethepower"?

Now, intellectually, I know that this young man was making a fair point. "I don't have the power" describes a common (indeed, ubiquitous) state of affairs. Still, such talk does get my dander up.

I read—and think and speak and write—about many, many things. Major issues in business. And beyond. (That's how I earn my living.) But this issue is different. *It's up-close and personal!* It gets right to the core of how I've lived my life ever since I was a "powerless" junior officer in the U.S. Navy in 1966 ... ever since I was a "powerless" new-kid-on-the-block consultant at McKinsey & Co. in 1974.

In each case, I reveled in my powerlessness. It was precisely the challenge (and the "cover"!) that I needed. I urge you to think about your "powerless" situation in the same way.

The Power of "Powerless" Thinking

"Getting Things Done" is not about formal "power" or official "rank." It is ultimately about ...

PASSION AND IMAGINATION AND PERSISTENCE.

Say you've got a Seriously Cool Idea. The very worst thing you can do—*the biggest waste of time in the world*—is to try to "sell" that idea "up the chain of command." Doing so will only remind you of how (officially) "powerless" you are. (De Gaulle didn't stick around and try to talk Petain out of executing him.)

The "chain of command"—what is that, anyway? It's a bunch of people who have been promoted for skillfully adhering to "the certified-pure way we do things around here." In other words: They are the Designated Guardians of Yesterday. For your purposes—as a "powerless" junior

talent

!

WOW projects for the "powerless"

YOU'RE NEVER TOO BOLD
Johann Wolfgang von Goethe: "Until one is committed, there is hesitancy, the chance to draw back. Concerning all acts of initiative (and creation), there is one elementary truth that ignorance of which kills countless ideas and splendid plans: that the moment one definitely commits oneself, then Providence moves, too. All sorts of things occur to help one that would never otherwise have occurred. ... Whatever you can do, or dream you can do, begin it. Boldness has genius, power, and magic in it. Begin it now."

type with a Seriously Cool Idea—the "chain of command" might as well be ... a chain gang.

Query: What constitutes a Seriously Cool Idea? Simple. It's something that runs directly counter to ... "the way we do things around here." That is, a Seriously Cool Idea is—by definition—a Direct Frontal Attack on the Holy Authority of Today's Bosses.

Hence, the power of the "powerless" lies in what I call "Boss-Free Implementation." Or: What "they" can't see, "they" can't kill!

What's Wrong with This Picture? Or: Reframe It!

There you are, low person on the organizational totem pole, "powerless" to create your own WOW Project. But look around. What projects—non-WOW projects, to be sure—are you involved in? Ask yourself: Can I *reframe* one of them in a way that lets me do ... under the radar ... Boss-Free Implementation of a Seriously Cool Idea?

My view: The answer is almost invariably "Yes!" Accordingly, I bid you to consider the following Reframers' Rules, as I call them.

Rule #1:

Never accept an assignment as given.

Only idiots accept assignments as given! Those who will change the world (in the smallest of ways, even) twist any assignment until it can be turned into a ... Seriously Cool WOW Project.

MY "EXCELLENCE" ADVENTURE

I really believe in this "power of the powerless" thing. After all, that's how I approached the research at McKinsey & Co. that led to the publication of *In Search of Excellence* (the offspring of which apparently accounts for about 50 percent of the firm's business these days).

My secret (and thus my stroke of great good fortune): NOBODY GAVE A DAMN. Hence I could scurry about pretty much as I pleased. I could recruit any Committed Junior Freaks I could find. And I did. One of those junior freaks became—well over a decade later, and long after I was "urged to seek other employment"— Managing Director of the Whole Shebang.

Rule #2:

You are never so powerful as when you're "powerless."

When are you truly hemmed in? When everybody is watching! Everybody views your slightest twitch through an electron microscope. But when you are Officially Powerless ... you are virtually free to dig into any assignment ... and Raise Hell at Will. "They" are effectively blind to your machinations.

Rule #3:

Every "small" project contains the DNA of the entire enterprise.

Perhaps this is the "real" secret-of-secrets: Every "small" project is a ... Perfectly Transparent Window ... on the Soul of the Organization, a far better window than "official policy." In sum: You don't need an *Officially* Big Project to attack a Very Big *Real* Opportunity.

The Army of WOW Credo: Always Volunteer

Opportunities! They are always (ALWAYS!) lying around. More often than not, they're lying around in the form of ... Crappy Jobs. Jobs that nobody else wants, seemingly for good reason.

talent

!

WOW projects for the "powerless"

RULES FOR THE "OVER-RULED"

Back before my own book on WOW Projects was available, my company used an unusual text in its WOW Project training. Title: *Rules for Radicals*. It was written 30-odd years ago by the tough Civil Rights and union-organizing militant Saul Alinsky.

The message: Getting Things Done in the Face of Conventional Wisdom is a Matter of Persistent Community Organizing ... a Matter of Engaging Passionate (and Putatively "Powerless") Others .

GET (UN)REAL

Azar Nafisi, author of the 2004 best-seller *Reading Lolita in Tehran*: "Never let reality get in the way of imagination."

I love that quote (which comes courtesy of Audi's "Never Follow" Web site).

Always
Volunteer.

But think again ... and follow the VFCJ Strategy.

That is: Volunteer For Crappy Jobs.

Yes, *volunteer*. In the Army, there used to be a credo: Never Volunteer. Don't step out or stand out. Hide within the infantry ranks, and you'll likely increase the odds of coming home safely. Well, that was the Old Army. In the New Army, every soldier is ... An Army of One.

Likewise, in the New Economy, you must ... Create Your Own Army of WOW. Which means: Volunteer! Even for those ... Crappy Jobs. *Especially* for those ... Crappy Jobs. Because Crappy Jobs let you take independent charge of things quickly and early in your tenure. Things that "nobody cares about" ... things that are out of sight and out of (the boss's) mind.

The pivotal question: Is that "unwanted" project a "throw-away task," a distraction to be "gotten out of the way"? Or is it a Stealth Opportunity to turn a "trivial" problem into ... a Seriously Cool Chance to address a Great Cultural Issue ... that strategically affects your entire organization?

Let's get down to cases:

Voluntary Contribution #1: Beyond "It's No Picnic."

Which is it? The "Oh-Shit-I-Wish-It-Were-Over Company Picnic"? Or: The "First Annual Seriously Cool Celebration of Our Incredible Staff"?

Nobody wants the job—the job of "boss" of the annual company picnic. But you say, "Aha! What an opportunity! Nobody wants this thing. Everybody hates it. But ain't it true that we do have a ... Seriously Cool Staff ... in our 73-person Telemarketing Department? Doesn't it make sense to Celebrate their Seriously Cool

Greatness? And what better opportunity than the dreaded ... Company Picnic?"

So you cobble together a little band of "powerless" but determined volunteers. You all throw Heart and Soul into what may be on the verge of becoming a ... WOW Project. You find some entertainers on the cheap. You discover untapped skills among staff. Friends of friends provide other resources. For two months, you let your "real work" slip. The powers-that-be think you're nuts ... that you're taking your eye off The Ball. ("The Ball" meaning ... Your Official Career.)

But the Dreaded Picnic becomes ... an Insanely Great Event! There is Buzz. Serious Buzz. "Powerless" you is "on the map." (Your betters were watching!) Plus, you gained the Unstinting Respect of 73 folks in the previously under-appreciated but vitally important telemarketing department. Plus, it was Fun! Plus, you added Members to your Network. ("It's all about the Rolodex, baby!")

Voluntary Contribution #2: Safety First.

Is it "Wrestle the damn safety manual into line with the nutty new occupational-safety regs"? Or: "Make an Advance in the All-Important War for Talent by figuring out how Safety Matters help to make this an ... Insanely Great Place to Work"?

Once more: Nobody wants the job. (To put it mildly.) But you see it as an ... Incredible Opportunity ... to Win a Major Battle in the Great War for Incredible Talent.

Voluntary Contribution #3: Process Makes Perfect.

Is it "Fix these bloody customer problems that have dogged the release of the new 2783B machine"? Or: "Work with a hotshot young GM on using Internet speed to gather customer input—not just after, but also before and during, the product-design process"?

"It's all about the Rolodex, baby!"

Yet again: Nobody wants the job. Nobody except you. Okay, by now you get the idea. Opportunities are where you see them. Power ... not official power, but the power of Initiative and Imagination ...is yours for the taking.

You just need to take it.

WOW CHOICE: FROM "CRAPPY" TO "COOL"

Like most things in life, the meaning of a project is all about ... attitude. Is it a chore, or is it a chance—a chance to do Something Great? How we answer that question says everything about who we are and how we see the world.

The way we respond to a "mere picnic" is a perfect snapshot of the degree to which we give a damn (OR DON'T) about our staff. That "mere social event" provides a better tip-off of our approach to fellow employees than 100 pages of turgid prose in an HR policy manual.

Likewise, the safety manual update provides a sparkling opportunity to highlight how much we care (OR DON'T) about the Overall Context in which Our People Work. And those "little" new-product problems are a Perfect Window on the way we Value Customers (OR DON'T).

Plays Well with Others

So success with several reframed crappy jobs has earned you Gold Stars ... and a flicker of recognition. But truth be told, you're still preoccupied with your own Seriously Cool Idea— and frankly not much closer to launching it on the world. As a young engineer, your power score is still low, and your discretionary budget is zero.

Is there any hope?

There's more than that: There's a Eureka Moment awaiting you.

To wit: Find a playmate!

What you need is one sympathetic, enthusiastic, piratical, conspiratorial friend. Yes, just one. (One is plenty. For now.)

You've done some research on, say, your radical notion of Totally Transforming Project

Management. You've done some serious reading. And you've chatted up some people who've tried similar ideas at other places.

Your excitement level rises. So, too, your frustration level. You desperately want to collar your boss and announce that you have figured out a way to ... Change the World.

Don't do it!
Resist the temptation!

Instead: Head to a company online chat room. Attend a company meeting. Start cold-calling to set up lunches with interesting people in the company you've gotten rumor of. In short, the time has come to take this Seriously Cool Idea ... and start talking it up with some Would-Be Seriously Cool Allies.

Another name that I like for this "playmate" strategy is ...

the F4 Approach: Find a Freaky Friend Faraway.

FREAK OUT: THE OUTSIDE-IN GAMBIT
The Freaky Friend does not have to be a colleague from your company. One of the best ways to innovate is to recruit somebody from a client organization. (A Cool Customer.)
Or somebody in a supplier company. (A Vivacious Vendor.)
Again: You have that Seriously Cool Idea. The "cool" part means that the "establishment"—including your company's hyper-conservative Crucial Customers (or Vaunted Vendors)—won't even consider the idea. So find a small, innovative customer (or vendor) instead and use that organization as your playpen.

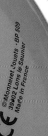

©Monnaret Jouets · BP 609
39402 Lons le Saunier
Made in France

talent

WOW projects for the "powerless"

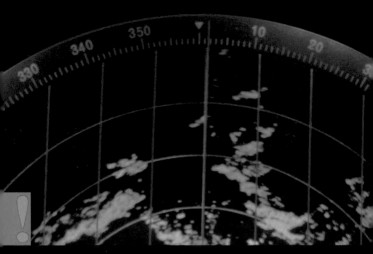

Eureka! You're closing in on Finding that first Freaky Friend Faraway.

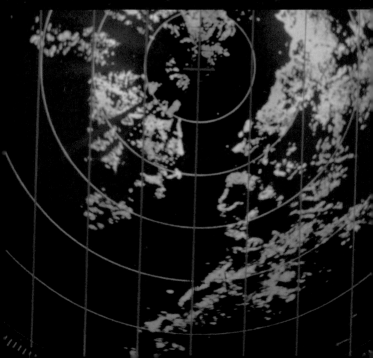

A (Play)Date With Destiny

Find a PLAYMATE

An example of the F4 (Find a Freaky Friend Faraway) Approach:

You have a colleague—call her Nancy—who runs a medium-sized engineering unit within a subsidiary of your company. Her office is a few hours' drive from the divisional HQ where you labor away as a Junior Dude on the Engineering Staff.

You already know Nancy slightly. The grapevine says she's aggressive and energetic, and willing to try damn near anything—as long as it's interesting. You drive out to meet her for coffee, and the two of you dive into conversation. You talk up your Seriously Cool Idea.

Nancy enthuses over your pitch. Particularly since she's now working on a project that has become stalled—and for which your Seriously Cool (and Potentially Subversive) Idea might be just the thing.

Nancy says that while she's not quite "in love with" your idea (that's your job!), she is "very intrigued" by it. She tells you that she'll mull over your approach, sound out some of her staff about it, and look into testing some version of it in her shop.

Eureka! (Redux.) You're closing in on Finding that first Freaky Friend Faraway.

Again: *One* is the critical number. One excited recruit at a time, at least in the beginning, at least until Dramatic Demos and Small Wins are in place.

talent

WOW projects for the "powerless"

OUT OF SIGHT?

Distance matters. Your goal must be to stay under the radar until your idea hits cruising speed. "Out of sight, out of mind" remains a potent axiom even in the Age of the Internet.

Fact: Most world-beating projects were incubated a long way from HQ, a place where intriguing ideas invariably get politicized and homogenized into submission. To this day, I believe that much of the success that Bob Waterman and I had in our "search for excellence" 20-odd years ago stemmed from our being in San Francisco—a full continent away from McKinsey's Corporate Shark Tank in Manhattan.

Try, Try Again: The Power of Prototyping

You're junior. You're "powerless." No vice-presidential chevrons on your sleeves. But you've got that Seriously Cool Idea. And you've found Nancy—that first Freaky Friend Faraway. What you need is ... a track record. A record of events-cum-stories that send a signal that "something's up."

There is one—and only one—way to hone your Seriously Cool Idea and get it ready for Prime Time. One and only one viable approach to creating a track record. And for that, I turn to innovation expert Michael Schrage.

Schrage spent the better part of a decade on what may seem like an obscure, dry-as-dust topic: *prototyping*. That is, the process by which enterprises move from abstract concept to concrete working model, and then put that model through its paces ... over and over again. Prototyping has its origins in manufacturing, but the idea goes way, way beyond that.

Schrage (who developed this thesis further in his book *Serious Play*) argues that excellence in Rapid Prototyping is the *chief* difference between organizations that innovate brilliantly ... and those that don't. "Effective prototyping," he writes, "may be the most valuable 'core competence' an innovative organization can hope to have."

Strong language. The message: *Become a Rapid Prototyping Maniac*.

Big "Wins" Come in Small Packages

Years (and years and years) ago, in my Ph.D. dissertation at the Stanford Business School, I coined another term for what I now call Rapid Prototyping. Namely: the "small win." That is, the wee "demo" whose success adds to your track record ... and thus to your credibility.

talent

! WOW projects for the "powerless"

IN THE "MEAN TIME"
Michael Schrage cites an interview with former Sony CEO Nobuyuki Idei, who claimed that rapid prototyping is the essential ingredient to Sony's extraordinary record of new product development. At Sony, according to Idei, the "Mean Time To Prototype" (the elapsed time between the glimmer of a new idea and a one-sixteenth-baked test of that idea) is a mere *five* working days.

Become a **Rapid Prototyping MANIAC.**

Who has the time for a
8,999-game losing streak?

Yes, that "small win," that "little test," that "successful prototype," shows that your Seriously Cool Idea isn't just a fantasy, after all. It shows that your Seriously Cool Idea may well become ... a Very Big Deal. An all-important entry on the credit side of your nascent track record. In fact, a giant and necessary step from Gleam in Your Eye to Dirt Under Your Fingernails. A catalyst for buzz that begins to make its way up the chain of command.

Nor does the "small win" even need to be a "win" in the obvious, conventional sense of the word. Sometimes a small win comes in the form of a "quick loss." That's certainly how Thomas Edison saw the matter. The Greatest Inventor of All went through some 9,000 experiments before he finally landed upon the right design for his incandescent bulb. Did he see the first 8,999 experiments as "failures"? Hardly! Each of those earlier "prototypes" was a Brilliant Demonstration of something that didn't work—in other words, a Clear Victory!

"Ouch," you shout. Who has the time for a 8,999-game losing streak? Fair enough, but the Edisonian "secret" is an Eternal Truth. We only win in the long run by getting out there—and getting bloodied—in the short run. As Churchill put it, "Success is the ability to go from one failure to another with no loss of enthusiasm."

THE REAL "FAIL-SAFE": FAIL QUICK

Variations on the theme of "quick loss":

A high-tech executive who attended a seminar of mine shared his philosophy: Fail. Forward. Fast.

IDEO founder and innovation guru David Kelley gives it another twist: Fail faster. Succeed sooner.

Glib? Perhaps.

Profound? Surely.

WOW POWER—TO THE POWER OF 10
Kevin Roberts, CEO of Saatchi & Saatchi Worldwide and author of a great book from 2004 (*Lovemarks*), offers a decalogue on "Strategy" that every "powerless" would-be talent start would do well to follow:

1. Ready. Fire! Aim
2. If it ain't broke, break it!
3. Hire crazies!
4. Ask dumb questions.
5. Pursue failure.
6. Lead, follow, or get out of the way.
7. Spread confusion.
8. Ditch your office.
9. Read odd stuff.
10. Avoid moderation.

PLAY!
INNOVATE!
FAST!

Let's Test Again: The Dance of Innovation

Rapid Prototyping turns out not to be about discrete "tests." It is ... a Way of Life. Think of it as a *dance*. With a particular series of steps and a particular rhythm. Think of it as ... the Dance of Innovation. It goes like this:

You get an idea. You run a (very) quick and (very) dirty test. That's great. But you've only begun. Now, after that first hair-brained test, you immediately sit down with your co-conspirators and you ask yourselves: "What happened? What can we learn from that test? What can we do differently next time?" And then you get on with that "next time" ... RIGHT AWAY. And so on. Again and again.

After a while, you get good at it. You develop ... a *rhythm*. And that's when innovation really starts to occur. Yes, your initial idea is Seriously Cool. (Don't let anyone tell you otherwise.) But it's just that—an idea. As yet, it is only potentially subversive. As Schrage astutely observes, the Real Work of Innovation comes with ... *the reaction to the prototype.*

True innovation is not about having a cool idea. True innovation is about what you learn when you actually test a potentially cool idea. The (big) idea here: You can't innovate until you have something tangible (a prototype) that you can ... PLAY WITH.

Play!

Innovate!

Fast!

Hence your goal: rapidly executed prototypes ... prototypes that may succeed or may fail ... but from which you reap Quick Learning and generate Growing Excitement and Growing Credibility. And, yes ... Growing Power.

talent

WOW projects for the "powerless"

ALL THE WORLD'S A ... PROTOTYPE

The arts have lots to teach us about innovation. Consider theater. We start by reading through the play. (Proto-Prototype.) Then we have slow walk-throughs. (Prototypes.)

Then we do bits and pieces of the prospective performance at full speed. (More prototypes.) Then we practice full scenes. (Yet more prototypes.) Then comes the dress rehearsal. (Mega-prototype.) Then we put on the play for real.

Such "serious play" is common in arts (and in sports). It is highly unusual in business— where we typically plan and plan, and meet and meet, before we ever do anything.

Power Suite: Tools for the Putatively Powerless

To review: You're in love with a Seriously Cool Idea. You want to turn it into a WOW Project. But ... you're a "junior person" and hence "powerless."

My advice:

DON'T SCREW AROUND.
START NOW.
FIND AN EXCUSE.
ANY EXCUSE.
DO SOMETHING.
DO ANYTHING.
GET GOING.
POSTHASTE.

More specifically: Take these steps (or some variation thereof):

1. You get passionate about a Seriously Cool and Subversive Idea.

2. You successfully resist blubbering to the boss about your idea. (Even if it's your Dad at a family-owned company.) (Especially if it's Dear old Dad.)

3. You express your passion about the idea with folks from hither or thither.

4. You find (or trip over) One Freaky Friend ... One Passionate Playmate.

5. With your One Passionate Playmate, you test and modify your idea in her Playpen.

6. You and your First Faraway Freak scour your networks for "line" folks who might be interested in "playing" with you at the next stage of the game.

7. Working with these new playmates, you concoct a rough and ready Rapid Prototyping schedule.

8. You start prototyping like a fiend.

9. You have a bunch of failures. You have a few successes. You learn ... a lot. You learn ... fast. You begin to accumulate a compelling track record. You sharpen your story.

10. You score some "small wins" and also get some quick learning ("small losses") under your belt.

11. You continue to resist the impulse to tell the boss about the project.

12. A freshly recruited Freaky Friend of your First Freaky Friend Faraway (call him a Premier Passionate Playmate) starts the Dance of Prototyping in his little bailiwick.

13. The Friend of the Friend unearths yet another Freaky Friend, maybe not quite so far away now, who wants to play with your now battle-tested idea. And so on ...

14. Meanwhile, you adjust and adjust and adjust. (Remember: Rapid Prototyping.)

talent

WOW projects for the "powerless"

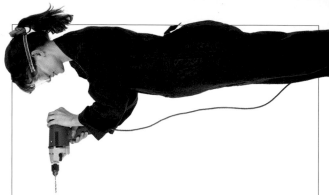

15. You start low-key "buzz building," letting word of Cool Small Wins trickle out—always giving Freaky Friends the credit. (Remember, Nancy is from line engineering. You're wet-behind-the-ears non-credible division staff.)

16. You begin nudging your growing Coven of Cool Converts to initiate a Major Proposal "up the line."

17. Before you know it, you are on the way to Surrounding the (Establishment) Bastards.

18. Now, and only now—flush with compelling data about successful "demos" by real line players—does your "pitch" get made to the Big Boss.

19. Note that, even now, *you* don't make the pitch! Remember: You are a Junior Staffer. Instead, you get those "real" line people—people who have been working successfully with Your Baby—to make the case for you.

(We don't have space here for a full-blown treatise on the Politics of Persuasion. But suffice it to say, in a perfect world, the boss has heard the "trickle-up" stories about your prototypes. You allow him to assume ownership and act as if he dreamed the whole damn thing up on his own. Hence he congratulates you on having read his mind. And signs off on a $4 million roll-out plan.)

20. And so it goes ... **Forever!**

TOP 10 TO-DOs

1. *Fight the power.* Or rather: *Be* the power. So you have no (formal) power. So what? Gandhi had no "power." Martin Luther King, Jr., had no "power." Yet they moved nations. They *were* power.

2. *Sign up.* Grab hold of those jobs that no one else wants—seemingly with good reason. Prove them wrong. Volunteer.

3. *Be above the frame.* Take that "crappy" job and ... *change it!* Reframe it into a project that holds forth the promise of WOW.

4. *Delve into your Day-Timer.* Check your calendar for *this week.* Find some task or duty on it (no matter how "small" or how "crappy") that you can transform a WOW project of your own.

5. *Play nice.* Advance your own private idea—your personal, "powerless" quest for WOW—by recruiting allies hither and yon. Call them Freaky Friends. Call them Playmates. Call them *now.*

6. *Raid your Rolodex.* Thumb through your list of contacts (or scroll through them on your PDA) in search of a Potential Playmate. Pick five candidates. Send five emails (or make five phone calls).

7. *Go to trial.* Move speedily from the Memo Stage to the Demo Stage of your project. Motto: Test, test, test (and test again).

8. *Win small.* Keep your eye on the Big Picture. But also treasure the Small Step Forward ... or Seeming Step Backward (aka "quick loss") ... that keeps you in the game and on your way.

9. *Spread the word* (softly). Resist the urge to sell your project before the Time is Ripe. As it begins to take off, start building buzz on the sly. Remember: To go over finish line, stay under the radar.

10. *Revel in "Irrelevance."* Make a virtue of the fact that no one takes you seriously. Imagine yourself as a Spy in the House of WOW, secretly plotting the overthrow of the Way Things Are Done.

COOL FRIEND: Ed Michaels

*Ed Michaels is a former director of McKinsey &
Company. In the 1990s, he led McKinsey's landmark
War for Talent study, which involved surveys of 13,000
executives at more than 120 companies, along with case
studies of 27 leading companies. With two McKinsey
colleagues, Helen Handfeld-Jones and Beth Axelrod, he
co-authored a book on the study,* The War for Talent
*(2001). Below are some remarks that he made about
the findings outlined in that book.*

* *

We have moved away from an industrial economy to
an information and services and high tech economy, in
which there are a lot more knowledge workers. And ...
studies suggest that the difference in value or output or
first quality productivity, whatever you call it, from a top
performer to an average or below average performer is
over 100 percent. Whereas in an assembly line it's
20 percent. So there are more knowledge worker jobs and
we now know that greater talent in those positions creates
more value than it did in the industrial revolution.

* *

[T]he supply of 24- to 45-year-olds in the United States
over the next 15 years is actually declining 10 to 12
percent, at the same time that the economy, presumably,
will be growing two, three, four, five percent. There just
aren't enough talented people to go around.

* *

Because of the supply and demand for talent, the power
has shifted from the companies, who used to be able
to say, "Hey, all you people line up for a job here. We'll
screen you carefully and one of you lucky 12 people will
get a job." The power has now shifted to the individuals.
And locating jobs is easier than ever, given sites like
hotjobs.com and monster.com. Also, there's no stigma to
changing jobs any longer.

* *

[T]he combination of those three things—more knowledge workers, not enough supply, and hence the related shift of the power away from companies to people—has created what we call "The War for Talent."

* *

Let's say you've got 30 people in your talent pool, and suppose the mix is 20 percent top performers, 60 percent average performers, and 20 percent under-performers. What if you can shift that mix to 40-50-10 or 50-50? The leverage in that is enormous.

* *

One of the real interesting facts that came out of our two massive surveys was that only 17 percent of the 12,000 managers we surveyed agreed that their companies even know who the strongest and weakest performers were!

* *

[W]hat skills are learnable, and which aren't? Conceptual ability IQ, for instance, is not something that can be developed beyond a certain age. The charisma that some people have is something that probably cannot be developed. ... But there are other skills: the skill of being candid, the skill of caring about people, the skill of being an effective mentor and coach. I think those functional and technical skills can be developed.

* *

When you talk about "development," ... most people think about training. Training is 10 percent of the development equation. Fifty percent is the sequence of jobs that you have, and 40 percent is the coaching and mentoring and candid feedback that you have or don't have. And these 12,000 managers not only told us that ... but they also told us that their companies were way under-delivering a sequence of stretch jobs and even more under-delivering coaching feedback and mentoring.

* *

It all starts with the fundamental belief that "Having a stronger talent pool is how I'm going to achieve my goals and be successful." And if I believe that, then it's got to be one of the two or three most important things that I do.

4

Bringing WOW Work
to Fruition:
The Sales25

Contrasts

Was	Is
"The Sales Department is down the hall."	"The Sales Department is right here!"
"Command and control"	"All sales, all the time"
A Supreme Leader who ... issues commands	A team leader who ... develops camaraderie
I was "assigned" to this task	I volunteered for this task
Leader says: "I'm in charge here!"	Leader shouts: "I'm here to sell this project."

!Rant

We are not prepared ...

We have too long depended on **"THE HIERARCHY"** to **"TAKE CARE OF US"** ... as long as we were doing a **"DECENT JOB."** • We must understand that in order to survive as Top-Flight Talent in this topsy-turvy world, we must all reinvent ourselves as ... **FIRST-RATE SALESPEOPLE.**

**NO "SALES MENTALITY" =
NO WOW PROJECTS =
NO SURVIVAL.**

PERIOD.

!Vision

I imagine ...

A 26-person project team. •
Members "belong to" 14 different
companies in 7 different countries ON
3 DIFFERENT CONTINENTS.

Most have not met more than
two or three of their cohorts. •
Yet **to get a difficult job done ... fast ...**
requires **ENERGY AND ENTHUSIASM** and
an utter **ABSENCE OF BOUNDARIES.**

Which means that Talent **Job No.1** is
**"INCLUSION, FACILITATION, MOTIVATION
... *AND* SALES."**

The WOW of Sales

Getting things done—whether you're a junior staffer in purchasing, a finance director, or POTUS (President of the United States)—is mostly a matter of "sales." That is, getting people ... *inflamed* ... about your ideas. Inducing them to ... sign on with you ... and then to stick with you ... through thin as well as thick.

Of all the small-t "talents" that make up big-T "Talent," the most indispensable talent—the one without which all others lose their luster—is the ability to Make a Sale. Talent that is worthy of the name knows how to sell: to sell products, perhaps, but more important ... to sell projects. And, above all, Talent knows how to sell itself. (Remember: You, the "Talent" in question, are a *brand*.)

Key point: *Every* project has "customers." Imagine that you're trying to bring "radical" change to a mere "business process" in finance. In particular, you have a Seriously Cool Idea for a new financial-reporting method for your division. The "users" in other departments who will benefit from that method—or feel put upon by it!—are your *customers*.

surround the BASTARDS!

No matter how "cool" your idea may be, those customers must become ... *enthusiasts* ... of your project ... if you are to make a Significant Impact. (No implementation, no impact. Period.) If you can garner ... Passionate Grassroots "Customer" Supporters ... then you've taken a massive step toward "surrounding the bastards." ("The Bastards" = The Big Bosses = Defenders

talent

! *the sales25*

of the Current Way of Doing Things. Hey, they've been eyeballing that familiar financial report, eyes half closed, for 10 years. Why should they want to change?)

You may well be a technical virtuoso. (That's why you came up with this Seriously Cool Idea in the first place!) But *now* it's time to sharpen your "soft" skills—to master the Rules of Sales and Politics. There are no other rules that matter nearly so much.

All the above is a long-winded way of saying:

WELCOME TO ...
THE AGE OF SALES

(that is, the "Age" that follows the Age of Hierarchy and Order Barking).

Bottom line: Leading any part of a WOW Project means selling ... up and down (and all around) the organizational ladder ... all the time.

The Sales25

I originally prepared the following collection of "rules" for a presentation to the sales leadership team of a several-billion-dollar high-tech company. The list draws on 30 years of experience, and, I believe, it applies as much to the individual contributor on a six-person WOW Project team in finance as it does to a high-powered "salesperson" in a "Sales Department."

Here goes ...

talent

the sales25

1. Know Your Product.

It's an obvious point, but well worth stating (and re-stating): *You've got to be smarter than hell about what you're peddling!* And the "secret" to product knowledge goes beyond attending the classes, beyond reading the literature, beyond training to do demos. True product knowledge is *deep* knowledge. "Straight knowledge" is a necessary jumping-off point, but no more than that.

Deep knowledge comes from finding every known factual—and editorial—comment about your product or service. Everything that's ever been said or written about it in print, on the Internet, wherever. For example, you should know about all "objections" raised in popular reviews of the product or service (and be able to answer each one, of course).

Deep knowledge also means developing your internal network: Make friends with (deep) designers and (deep) engineers in your product development department, and encourage them to share the "real story behind the product"—along with the product's significant features and (yes) hidden shortcomings.

When it comes to developing product knowledge, remember: *More, more, more.* And, more important: *Deeper, deeper, deeper.*

In sum: He or she who has the largest appetite for Deep Knowledge wins.

2. Know Your Company.

Another truism (which doesn't mean that you can ever afford to forget it): You're selling your company as much as—or more than—you are selling a product or service.

You need to understand, cold and in-depth, all of the pertinent procedures and functions within your organization: finance, logistics, customer support, engineering, manufacturing. Be prepared to deal with any query from a customer.

But more than that: Be ready to use that fabulous internal network you've developed! Guides and mentors in every (EVERY!) critical part of your company! Colleagues who will teach you and act as your liaison to those other departments! That network, in turn, will grease the way to easier customer relations.

3. Know Your Customer.

Here again, you must become a research fanatic. Scour the footnotes in financial analysts' reports. Scour the Web. Fact: As never before, there is an incredible amount of Good Stuff available. Beyond that, you may be able to find people in your company who worked for your customer's company—or people at one of your vendors who worked for your customer's company. Or call an old college chum who worked there.

The goal: *Get to know the "corporate culture" of your customer's enterprise.* This learning process never stops! You need to know, and know cold, the "politics" of your customer's decision-making structures.

Getting to know the customer also means getting to know the individuals you will deal with. Any form of legitimate intelligence—including (especially) personal tidbits—is worthwhile. Advice: Until your "intelligence work" on all these issues is well on its way, don't even *think* about making that first customer call.

4. Love the Politics.

Axiom: All sales is politics. "Politics" ... meaning "the way people work with one another to get things done."

If you don't like—no, make that "love"—politics, you're going to be a crappy salesperson!

To be sure, politics can be frustrating and infuriating. But I've discovered that most people who are "frustrated" or "infuriated" by "politics" just don't cotton on to the facts of life of the political game. One person's "mind-melting frustration" with "politics" is another person's "exciting human puzzle."

talent

the sales25

In short, loving the "fray" per se—all the internal to-ing and fro-ing within your own company, your customer's company, and key vendors' companies—is essential to sales success.

"POLITICAL" RALLY

A "hard sell" point: If you don't love politics … if "politics" is a nasty word in your book … then don't even think about pursuing WOW in anything you do. Remember:

No politics, no implementation.

No implementation, no WOW.

---

5. Respect Your Competitors.

And when I say "respect" competitors, I mean respect them … *religiously*. You may hate their guts. Maybe with good reason. (Hey, they screwed you out of a sale! Or so you believe.) No matter.

DON'T BAD-MOUTH COMPETITORS. PERIOD.

Nothing makes you look smaller than dissing a legitimate competitor. The goal—the only goal—is to demonstrate why your product or your service is better for this customer than the other guy's product or service … and why your company is the better company to deal with.

There is no greater blessing than an extraordinary competitor. (Every day, the folks at UPS should mentally tip their hat to the folks at FedEx. And vice versa.) Great competitors keep you on your toes! Alas, none of us improves without having somebody who pushes us.

TAKE OUT THE TRASH TALK

What goes for competitors also goes for your fellow project-team members. In trying to get things done, you will get "jerked around" by dolts in this department or that. Live with it! Do not trash-talk your colleagues. If you do, "word" will get out … and your reputation will become that of a "whiner," not a "doer."

Recently, I read a story about change consultant Norman Guitry. He starts his presentation by saying, "All you need to know about mental health can be summed up in only two words." Then he proceeds to a whiteboard and writes: DON'T BELITTLE. His mighty mantra: "Don't ever, ever make people feel small."

Amen! Don't belittle others. And don't "be … little" yourself.

Bottom line: Sales depends on … R-E-S-P-E-C-T.

---

6. Wire Your Customer's Organization.

Develop close, congenial relationships at all levels and within all functions of your customer's enterprise. A "sale" … whether it happens in a formal sales transaction or on a project team … is often "made" four levels down from where it officially takes place.

Example: Junior staffer Mary Smith is responsible for "researching CRM applications in mortgage banking." Any business that you, as a CRM (Customer Relationship Management) vendor, do with her company must go through Mary's boss's boss's boss, who will have the "big meeting" with a Big Boss at your company and "ink the final deal." But Mary's report is decisive. So is the opinion of Richard, Mary's equally junior colleague, who "knows the real scoop on CRM reliability." Finding and courting the Marys and Richards is not easy. But that's what you must do if you want that sale. Think Mary. Think Richard. Forget "rank."

7. Wire *Your* Organization.

Key point: Your customer is buying not so much a widget as a Widget Provision and Support Experience. So: The more you can bring to bear … All of the Multi-Faceted Talent in Your Company upon that Experience … the better your odds of winning a sale and, better yet, a repeat sale. The same thing goes for all the Talent in your Critical Vendor Companies.

talent

the sales25

SIX DEGREES OF PREPARATION

Wiring an organization is a deeply human endeavor. But technology is fast becoming available that makes "wiring" a little something more than a metaphor. As reported in an August 2004 article in *Forbes*, companies like Spoke Software and Visible Path are coming out with digital tools that help salespeople and others figure out who knows whom—and how well— within a given company's ecosystem. The software measures such things as e-mail and phone traffic, and uses sophisticated algorithms to judge how closely linked various folks are to other folks.

Freaky? Yes.
Surprising? No.
(Not in 2004.)

Get to know that "talent." (That is: all of the "talent" throughout your supply chain.) *Wire* that talent. Make it—make them—connect for your customers.

WORK THE STAFF

During my tour in the White House, I learned a big lesson in "wiring the organization"—the organization being, in this case, the United States Congress. I needed Congressional help to execute my agenda. Lots of people in my position would move heaven and earth to "get five minutes" with a Representative.

Those were the fools. The wise ones, my mentor taught me, would get to know the junior staffers who did the Representative's leg work on a given issue. Over the long haul, the odds of success were directly proportional to "hours spent" with those "unimportant" junior staffers.

---

8. Never Over-Promise.

You want to win the sale. Your chief competitor is hungry—indeed, ferocious. You feel an overwhelming temptation to shave a few days off the promised delivery time. A little voice inside you says, "Hey, the factory will figure it out."

Well ... DO NOT LISTEN TO THAT LITTLE VOICE.

As a salesperson, you are always "out front" ... **alone** at the battle's edge. Your future is *always* at stake. And it is always totally dependent on your ... Trustworthiness.

My advice: Even if it costs you a sale now and then ... always *under*-promise. Add a couple of days here and there to increase the odds of "making target." (Invariably, at some point, the "yogurt" does hit the fan!) In the long haul, being the courier of pleasant surprises beats being the constant bearer of ill tidings.

Try this for a personal credo: WINNING SALESPEOPLE ARE ROUTINELY AHEAD OF SCHEDULE!

BE A BAD-NEWS BEARER

Here's a simple formula to follow when the yogurt does hit the fan: COMMUNICATE LIKE A MANIAC!

On one hand, the worst thing you can do is fail to communicate bad news that's clearly on the horizon ... in the juvenile hope that it will just "go away." On the other hand, passing on a rumor of bad news that does not actually materialize can work in your favor. (You come across as ... a Problem Solver.)

WINNING
SALESPEOPLE
ARE ROUTINELY
AHEAD
OF SCHEDULE.

9. Sell the Solution.

Sell only by ... Solving Specific Problems ... and by creating Identifiable Profit Opportunities. Great salespeople don't just sell "widgets." (Even "damn-good widgets.") They sell solutions. (Damn-good solutions.)

Ask yourself, at every stage of the sales process, "Is this a 'product sale' or a 'solution sale' that will get me written up in the trade press?"

Every sales pitch you make should boil down to this and only this: "Our product solves *these* specific problems, creates *these* unimaginably incredible opportunities, and will make *this* huge amount of money. Here is exactly *how*."

To paraphrase the marketing gurus, one doesn't sell a "Rolex watch." One sells "what it feels like to be a Rolex wearer." That's obvious. Or it should be. And what holds for Rolex holds for every sale ... including the internal "sale" of your "business-process redesign project."

"Solutions" Mantra: *Idiots sell Rolexes. Geniuses sell The Rolex Lifestyle.*

10. Ask for Help (and Put Pride Aside).

As you work to solve a customer's problem, to expand a customer's opportunity, to deepen a customer's experience ... draw on every possible resource. "Resources" means "people." Including mortal enemies.

Example: Once upon a time, you had a lousy experience with Jack Jones, a services vendor. And you're still pissed off about it, four years later. But now you have a Client—and Jack Jones is the perfect "consultant" to help you add credibility to your pitch to that Client.

So: *GET OVER IT.*

CALL JACK. SIGN HIM UP. BEG HIM TO BE PART OF THE DEAL.

Inspired selling involves bringing to bear the absolute best resources available to create the best outcome imaginable for a Client. And it's your job to muster those resources—even if you are less than charmed by some of the "resource providers."

**Idiots sell Rolexes.
Geniuses sell The Rolex Lifestyle.**

11. Live the Brand Story.

Your company sells a "story." A story about "the way it is to do business with us." A story about "our vision," the "experience we offer," "our dream." In short, a story about our ... "BRAND."

Know that story cold! Tell it! Use it! Make it your own! I'm not urging you to be a mindless suck-up to the company line. I am reminding you that in the best companies, Brand Value amounts to hundreds of billions of dollars in value. Thus, if you can't "buy into the brand promise," then you probably shouldn't stick around.

Give the brand promise your own twist and your own turn, to be sure. Yes, personalize the hell out of it. But take full advantage of the "goodwill" your company has built up over the decades.

> **FACING "UP"**
>
> *You are your brand. Your face is the face of the brand. Ergo, make that face a brave and happy one. Smile!*
>
> *A Chinese proverb, as quoted in* The Art of Achievement, *by Tom Morris: "A man without a smiling face must not open a shop."*
>
> *Nor should he "open" a sales pitch.*

12. Celebrate the "Good Loss."

A "good loss" is a brave and brash effort that ... for whatever reason ... doesn't come to fruition. (Yet.) Particularly in madcap times, and especially over the long haul, a good loss (aka "excellent failure") can be far better than a "lousy win" (aka "mediocre success").

A lousy win is one that brings in a few more bucks for doing the Same Old Stuff. A good loss comes from repositioning a product or service to create a potentially awesome experience ... one that your Client isn't quite nervy enough for. (Yet.)

Take the "good loss" idea too far, and you'll have nothing to show for it but hubris. Nonetheless, I urge you to err—ever-so-slightly—in the direction of celebrating that good loss. Push your Clients beyond their comfort zones; if you don't, you're going to lose them to an upstart, perhaps sooner than you think.

13. Make Every Problem Your Problem.

If anything goes wrong in your dealings with a Client, you're screwed, right? What follows is obvious: *All customer problems are your problems!* So: Don't ever— EVER!—blame a late delivery on the "logistics people."

YOU ARE THE SALESPERSON. YOU "ALONE" ARE THE LEAD DOG IN REPRESENTING YOUR COMPANY TO THE CUSTOMER. TO THE CUSTOMER, YOU *ARE* THE COMPANY. ERGO, IF SOMETHING WENT WRONG, *YOU* SCREWED UP. NOT THE "LOGISTICS PEOPLE."

Which is not to say that you don't have the right to be pissy with the people in logistics if they did, in fact, screw up. You just can't transmit that ire to the Client. The instant you do, your reputation goes down the drain.

Remember: They signed a deal with you, not with some abstract "company."

14. Take Full Responsibility.

You are the customer's "point-person" for your entire enterprise. You make your real money from Repeat Business. And Repeat Business depends only somewhat on the product or service that you offer. It depends mostly—fundamentally—on the Seriously Cool Continuing Experience that customers have of working with you. And that Experience will be absolutely, positively fabulous to the extent that you purposefully *orchestrate* it.

Fact is, salespeople make their sustaining commissions far more by orchestrating Seriously Cool Client Experiences that emanate from *all* departments in their company, and throughout their supply chain, than they do by presenting a "torrid" sales pitch. Think of yourself as an Orchestra Conductor.

Repeat after me, then: "I am fully responsible for making my whole organization and its partners respond aggressively and harmoniously to the needs and wishes of my customer."

I am *fully* Responsible

talent

the sales25

HOARD=
LOSE

SHARE=
WIN

15. Don't Hoard Information.

Some salespeople do their best to "keep the Client to themselves"—to control all contact between the Client and their company.

Dumb. Dumber. Dumbest.

You do *not* want the Client to be slavishly dependent upon you. You want the Client to have a Scintillating Experience with you—*and* with everyone in your orbit. To feel "at home" with your organization. To have close, usable contacts in your engineering, logistics, and finance departments.

When trouble arises and you're not available, you want the Client to have a fully loaded Rolodex of people within your company who can fix the glitch.

I things go well, particularly after a glitch, you will get the credit. And things will go well, over the long haul, precisely to the extent that you have created a network of relationships that give the Client "family" access to every element of your company.

Hoard = Lose.
Share = Win.

talent

the sales25

16. Walk Away from Bad Business.

Don't be a quitter. Don't give up when the first flies appear in the ointment. But don't hang in there ... and in there ... and in there ... and sacrifice your calendar and your soul in perpetuity, in order to make your numbers.

Be very clear on this: THERE *IS* SUCH A THING AS "BAD BUSINESS."

When you find people in a customer organization to be untrustworthy, when the game-playing required to make a sale rises far above the normal push-and-pull of politics, when business becomes positively painful, you may well need to make a graceful (or not-quite-so-graceful) exit.

I'm not advising you to be "holier-than-thou." Politics *is* normal. Compromise *is* eternal. But there *are* limits.

For example:

Don't work with people who are dishonest.

Don't work with people who don't keep their word.

Don't work with people who care only about themselves.

Don't work with jerks.

LIFE IS TOO SHORT.

HONOR THY FUTURE

Remember: Nobody on his or her deathbed says, "I made my numbers 73 quarters in a row." No, when you're on your deathbed, you'll talk about Peak Experiences ... experiences of which you are particularly proud. Sure, most of those "peaks" involve friends and family. But many of them involve super-cool things that you've done in your professional life. And those things are invariably honorable.

---

17. Don't Whine About Price.

It's okay to lose business on price. *I've* lost business on price. (Numerous times.) You don't enjoy it, and it's fair to bitch now and again to the controller about the "insane margins" that he's trying to milk from an "ordinary" product or service. And yet ... one of the surest signs of a salesperson-going-nowhere is *continual* complaining about "losing sales on price."

Here's why: Again, what you're selling is no "ordinary" product or service. You are selling an Opportunity ... a Solution ... an Experience ... a Dream To Be Fulfilled. All of which still may not justify a 50 percent premium over an excellent competitor; but it damn well ought to justify some kind of premium!

In a world where "services added" are becoming more and more significant, the only game in town is to "Add an Awesome Armload of Intangibles" that will allow you to charge a healthy premium for what you are offering.

Bottom line: Those who say, "It's all a price issue," suffer from rampant immaturity and a shrunken imagination.

18. Don't Give Away the Store ... to Get a Foot in the Door.

Yes, be flexible! Yes, go the extra mile! But ... be careful! I have seen far too many cases of salespeople talking their organization into absurd compromises in order to get the "first sale" with some "big Client." These over-eager, pedal-to-the-metal salespeople always say the same thing: "Let's do it just this once. After that, we'll be able to get our normal margin."

In your dreams!

Remember: The line between "loss leader" and "lead loser" can be ... diaphanously thin.

Message: Once (perceived as) a sucker, forever a sucker.

19. Respect Upstarts (the *Real* Enemy).

The real enemy these days, over the medium to long term, is rarely your "chief competitor." It's more likely to be the competitor-that-doesn't-make-it-onto-your-radar-screen ... but that really does have a Seriously Better Idea

talent

!

the sales25

that will nail you to the wall over the next several years. That is, if you are not exceedingly alert.

Think Microsoft 20 years ago. Or Wal*Mart 20 years ago.

"Knowing the industry" means having good antennae out for the "little guys" that may not be little too much longer. Toward that end, make sure that your Extended Personal Network includes a few savvy venture capitalists who can feed you the "buzz" on what's coming next. (They may be wrong. But they will be unfailingly *interesting*. And they will keep you in fighting trim.)

IF YOU CAN'T BEAT 'EM ...

Another option: Give those upstart competitors a break. Work with them. Ask them to become part of the product-service-experience "package" that you offer to customers.

Far better to co-opt an emerging star as an "alliance partner" now than to see them become a major rival later.

---

20. Seek Cool Customers.

The "obvious" sales targets are almost always the biggest, most established ones. There is obviously some logic to such an approach. But in a time of dramatic change, it is utterly imperative that your customer portfolio include a significant share of "leading-edge" companies—folks that are pursuing *tomorrow's* flavors of excellence *today*.

You—you, the salesperson, and your company—are as "cool" as your customer portfolio is "cool."

It's that simple!
And that hard!

Message: Be *religious* in the evaluation of your Customer Portfolio. Ask yourself: Does my list of customers and prospects have a high enough … Weird Quotient … to provide me with a genuine bead on the (inevitably) Weird Future?

21. Talk "Partnership."

The word "partnership" is way overused. My advice: Use it anyway. Obsessively. (Hey, if the cliché fits …)

Why do I insist on using that word? Because what you are selling … no matter "what" you are selling … is just that: a partnership. A Virtual, Encompassing Web of Colleagues and Vendors who Devote their Herculean Efforts to Creating Opportunities for your Beloved Client.

Your job as a salesperson is to bring to bear—in a seamless fashion—the full power and imagination of your company's entire supply chain.

Sounds like a "partnership" to me.

So I mean it: USE THE DAMN WORD. "PARTNERSHIP."

22. Send Thank-You Notes!

A half-dozen years ago, I wrote a "summa" on implementation. Some 50 ideas. No.1 on the list:

DON'T FORGET YOUR THANK-YOU NOTES!

Obvious point (all too often honored in the breach): Sales is a RELATIONSHIP business. And a potent "tool" in the relationship game is a kind word. In other words: a thank-you note.

talent

the sales25

YOU ARE WHO YOU SELL TO
Big point: Hanging out with exciting, innovative people automatically makes *you* more exciting and more innovative—and keeps you ahead of the curve.

Call it "Automatic Innovation."

Whatever you call it, make sure that it's working for you. Because the converse is also true: Having dull customers … customers that never

challenge you except on price … will lead you to provide dull "solutions" and dull "experiences."

For more, see Chapter 5: "Thinking Weird: The Transcendent Talent."

Thank-you notes. Send them by the truckload.

The note of appreciation to the "Big Guy" who made time on his calendar for you is one thing. And important. But more important over the long haul: notes to people several rungs down the ladder, people who went a "little bit out of their way" to advance your cause.

Another rule of thumb: At least 50 percent of your thank-you notes should go to people *inside* your company—"unsung" people who help create better *experiences* (remember: that's what you're selling) for your customer.

Oh, and while I'm at it: Remember birthdays. Send birthday cards. And flowers when appropriate. "Little touches" are *never* little.

CAPITAL IDEA

I had a boss in Washington years ago. Insanely busy. But, on Day One of working with him, I observed that he closed his office door at about 7 p.m. for a half-hour.

A nip of Chivas Regal? Hardly.

He religiously spent those 30 minutes dictating (that's what we did back then) a dozen or more simple "thank-yous" to people he'd met during the day. People who had "gotten him a meeting" with someone he needed to see, or who had made a supportive comment when he really needed it.

Result (no overstatement): He had a slavish network of devotees throughout D.C. (aka Den of Cynicism).

---

23. Make Your Customer a Hero.

When you look across the table at your customer, think religiously and repeatedly to yourself: "How can I make this dude or dudette rich and famous? How can I get him or her promoted?"

It's not enough to focus on making the customer's *organization* "successful." Yes, that's clearly the long-term goal. But the practical, near-term imperative is to make a Solid Gold Hero (or Heroine) out of the *Individual* who is responsible for buying (and using) your product or service.

Consider: I am not in the "widget-selling business." *I am in the "Hero- (Heroine-) Making Business."*

"Companies" don't buy "things" from other "companies." Rather: *Individuals* buy *Successful Relationships* from other *Individuals*.

24. Keep Your Slides Simple.

If you're in sales (and again, if you're in the WOW Project Business, you're in the Full-Time Sales Business), sooner or later you drag out Ye Olde PowerPoint presentation. So: Keep those bloody presentation slides lean and full of meaning!

As noted, this Sales25 discussion stems from a presentation that I made to salespeople at a major tech company. As part of my prep work, I reviewed some of their presentations. And I was ... appalled. This is a company that peddles some great products. But each of their slides had way too much stuff on it.

Is it just my age? Am I just too old to see the fine print? No, damn it! The point of a presentation is to persuade ... not to perplex.

talent

the sales25

SETH SPEAKS—*VERY* BRIEFLY

Consider the immortal words of Seth Godin: "If you can't describe your position in eight words or less, you don't have a position."

THE LOYAL "WE"

Here's a trick I picked up long ago at McKinsey & Co.: Always use the word "we." In talking with customers, say, "We will take this approach ..."

Sure, it's a "trick." But the person you end up tricking (in the best sense of that word) is yourself!

Again: Every WOW Project is a ... partnership! A "we" thing.

SLIDE RULES

Don't let your slide show become a side-show. Here are a few basics on keeping the pith in your pitch:

- Keep it clear.
- Keep it simple.
- Declare your benefits.
- State your case.
- Tell your (COMPELLING) "story."
- Sit down.
- Shut up.

25. Aim to Change-the-Damn-World!

Selling is ... Cool. Very Cool. I really do believe, when I hawk my "wares" (when I present a seminar or write a book), that I'm doing more than buttering the bread and paying the property taxes. While I don't think I routinely change the world for large numbers of people, I know that I give a damn about what I'm doing—that I'm excited about delivering my product-service-experience.

talent

the sales25

Note well this *cri de coeur* offered by Apple Computer boss Steve Jobs: "Let's make a dent in the universe."

I think the notion that selling can be ... "universe-denting" ... is what keeps us motivated, and able to look at ourselves in the mirror.

We Are All Salespeople Now

Want to get my dander up? Try saying, "Hey, I'm a finance guy. I don't 'do' sales."

No! No! No!

Success = Sales Success. Everywhere. Period. We're all in sales. All the Time.

TOP 10 TO-DOs

1. *Case ... the joint.* *Your* joint, I mean. List five key "players" within your company. For each person, write a Sales Profile: What motivates him/her? How can we make him/her a hero or heroine?

2. *Case ... your competition.* Imagine that your company's prime competitor hired you today—and insisted that you go on a sales call tomorrow. How would you make that pitch? You should know "the other guy" well enough to make it *right now.*

3. *Case ... your presentation.* Pull up your latest (biggest, most important) slide show. Prune it *ruthlessly* of that which is superfluous. Order it *rigorously* according to the Logic of the Sale.

4. *Love ...* Embrace the politics that is *endemic* to sales work. Revel in it. Yes, it's messy. Yes, it's ... What You Do.

5. *Live ...* Embody the Brand Story that you seek to sell to the world. After all, at "the end of the day," that is what customers really buy.

6. *Own ...* Take (total) responsibility for every nuance of every interaction between your company and your customer. Mantra (again): *All customer problems are your problems!*

7. *Respect ...* Treat everyone (customers, colleagues, competitors) with honor. Remember: You can be a hero only by making *them* heroes.

8. *Walk ...* Be ready to abandon a sale or a prospect if the "cost" (financially, psychically) gets too high. Respect your Talent. And stay away from those who don't.

9. *Thank ...* Send out thank-you notes *promiscuously.* Tip: Block out three hours on your calendar each week for writing them.

10. *Sell ...* Nurture within yourself an Unmitigated Sales Ethos. You must sell your product (externally). You must sell your project (internally). You must sell your *Talent* (everywhere).

COOL FRIEND: Robert Sutton

*Robert Sutton, Professor of Management Science
and Engineering at the Stanford Engineering School,
is co-director of the Center for Work, Technology,
and Organization. Sutton, who lives in Menlo Park,
California, is the author of* **Weird Ideas That Work:
11½ Practices for Promoting, Managing, and Sustaining
Innovation** *(2001). Below are some remarks that he
made about the "weird ideas" in that book.*

* *

If you want to have an organization or a group of people
that keeps breaking from the pack, you need to have
variation and ideas that are floating around the group or
the company—wide variations—and you need to have
people who have what I call "vu jadé," which is the
opposite of *déja vu*. It's this ability to keep seeing the
same old thing as brand new.

* *

[M]ost managers, most of the time, are managing
routine stuff. And when you show them things that are
empirically based and are proven to enhance innovation,
it looks downright weird. Hence you have ideas in [my]
book such as "Hire 'Slow Learners' (of the Organizational
Code)." Why? Because you need people who see the
world differently than most people in the company and
who bring in varied ideas.

* *

[Y]ou should reward failure. Well actually, I don't think
you should reward failure among people who are learning
routine tasks like surgery or flying an airplane, because
you can identify the difference between success and
failure very reliably, and there's a right and a wrong way
to do it. And you don't want doctors experimenting on you
when they're doing a routine operation, an appendectomy.
You really don't.

But then there's the percentage of the time—and
the percentage will vary from industry to industry and

company to company—where it's necessary to go into this mode of being innovative. And then you have to do things like reward a high failure rate.

* *

My favorite weird idea is *Do something that will probably fail, and then convince everybody around you that success is certain.* And this is how the best venture capitalists and the best product development managers work. ... [I]t's a paradox, but it's how Silicon Valley works. It's an incredible model of self-delusion.

The reason you want to do something that will probably fail is that if you're doing something that will succeed, by definition you're imitating something that's proven. When you define innovation, it's going to be an imitation of the past. ... So, if you want learning, and in this case, innovation, you've got to accept some failure rate. And most venture capitalists, most people who do product development in big organizations, know this.

Mary Murphy-Hoye does a lot of IT research at Intel. She leads a team and she'll criticize people for not having a high enough failure rate. She says, "If you're not going to fail eight out of ten times, we're doing something wrong."

* *

[T]he most well-proven motivational tool on earth, and the cheapest, is the self-fulfilling prophecy. If someone is convinced that they're wonderful and they'll succeed, their odds of actually succeeding go way up.

* *

People who are like us, who agree with us, see the world in the same way, have the same training, the same background, those are the people who we automatically and unconsciously like. The logic of hiring people who we don't like, who make us uncomfortable, is that they very often will be people who have different ideas than we do. ... I don't think you should hire zillions of them, because if everybody hates everybody it'll be, like, too much warfare. But you want to have people who see the world differently.

5

Thinking Weird:
The Transcendent Talent

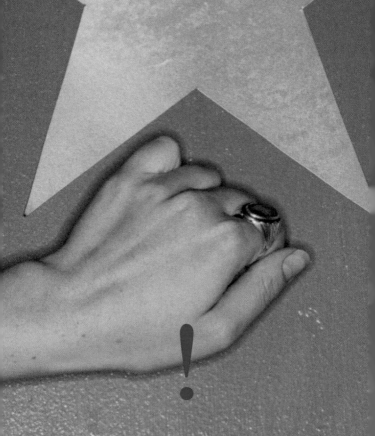

Contrasts

Was	Is
"Be ahead of the pack"	"Be ahead of the curve"
Get big fast: *"Size will defend us"*	Get a clue: "Size is no defense"
Maximize revenue by *focusing on a few* *big customers*	Maximize innovation by seeking out "strange" small customers
Benchmark against *"industry leaders"*	Benchmark against leading-edge firms
"Strategic" suppliers	Fringe suppliers
Reliable employees	Rambunctious employees
Hire the guy (gal) from *a prestigious school*	Hire the guy (gal) with a freaky portfolio
Passive board of directors	Pushy board of directors
Acquisitions: *buying bulk*	Acquisitions: buying innovation
"Safety-first" partners	"Risk-ready" partners
Playing it safe *("Cover all the bases")*	Playing it "weird" ("Burn all the ships")

!Rant

We are not prepared ...

WE CHAMPION INNOVATION. But then **we roll over and play dead** when a giant customer "urges" us to cancel or dumb down a risky new product that would upset the status quo. • **WE BEG FOR "MORE RISK TAKING." But then we videotape the "be daring" speech** featuring the boss in a Brooks Brothers suit, sitting behind an old oaken desk. • **WE EXHORT PEOPLE TO "GET WITH THE NEW TECHNOLOGIES." But then we freeze technology spending and require people to work with only "safe" vendors.** • (No wonder the "innovative organization" remains a chimera.)

!Vision

I imagine ...

A sales team that exerts as much energy to land **"THE STRANGE ACCOUNT"** as it does to land **"the Big Account."**

A hiring manager who says to interviewees, **"Describe the weirdest project you've ever undertaken, and how you lived to tell the tale."**

A purchasing manager who looks for suppliers who will not just fill Ongoing By-the-Book Needs, **but also present EMERGING OFF-THE-WALL OPPORTUNITIES.**

A CEO who insists that his board of directors include, along with the usual yes-men, **a goodly allotment of freaks—men and women who can't say "YES" without also saying "BUT ..."**

With a Little Help From My (Freaky) Friends

Along about 1984, I was stuck in a rut. My thinking was mired in the big-company theory and practice that I'd acquired at McKinsey & Co.

Then I got lucky. I met Frank Perdue, of Perdue Farms. And Roger Milliken, of Milliken & Co. And Bill and Vieve Gore, of W.L. Gore. And Tom Monaghan, of Domino's Pizza. And Les Wexner, of The Limited. And Don Burr, of People Express. And Anita Roddick, of The Body Shop.

I began to hang out with those and other feisty, we-can-change-the-world-and-damn-well-are-changing-it-and-isn't-that-a-kick characters. And guess what? Their spirit rubbed off on me. I was dragged into their quirky world.

And I've never looked back!

Along the way, I picked up a hard lesson: INNOVATION IS EASY.

Call me insane. I can handle that. But kindly hear me out. "Innovation"—the talent that makes all other talents relevant, the *sina qua non* of achieving excellence in a disruptive age— is easy. Not hard.

INNOVATION IS EASY

Fundamental proposition: *Hang out with weird ... and you will become more weird. Hang out with dull ... and you will become more dull.*

Could it really be that simple? I think so.

Though I have often been called an "organizational change consultant," I don't much believe in change. I don't much believe that launching a "strategic initiative" or creating a "brilliant training program" will suddenly cause people to lose their fear of failure, to become entrepreneurial, or whatever.

What I do believe is that if I can force myself into contact with "strange stuff" ... then that strange stuff will drag me, willingly or not, toward something new and thrilling, something weird and wonderful. I will change because of one and only one thing: I've been forced to!

The "Big" Problem: Poor Little Rich Company

In 2002, *Advertising Age* reported that domestic sales are declining in 20 of Procter & Gamble's 26 major product categories—including 7 of the top 10 categories.

Staggering!

What's the reason? Some analysts point to what they call the "billion-dollar problem": Given P&G's enormous size, the company rarely looks at a new product opportunity unless it has humongous potential. And in this case, "humongous" means ... about a billion bucks.

But therein lies a problem. Anything with "demonstrated" billion-dollar potential is, almost by definition, "more of the same"—more of the same kind of product, sold in mostly the same way to the same kind of people whom P&G has sold to in the past. In times of change, big companies—devoted to over-sized products aimed at over-sized customers, enamored of "me-too" focus groups—are doomed to the prospect of waddling after slow growth.

Simple and oft-demonstrated fact from the world of world-flipping innovation: Things that alter the world invariably enter by the side door. A small group of pioneering customers ("early adopters"), paired with a pioneering vendor, act as flag bearers and trailblazers for the rest of the world.

talent

!

thinking weird

SMALL IS BANKABLE
Seth Godin, writing in *Fast Company:* "Think small. One vestige of the TV-industrial complex is a need to think mass. If it doesn't appeal to everyone, the thinking goes, it's not worth it. ... Think of the smallest conceivable market and describe a product that overwhelms it with its remarkability. Go from there."

Disruptive Criticism: Being Safe and Sorry

The most articulate spokesman for the perils of "playing it safe" is TBWA/Chiat/Day CEO Jean-Marie Dru. He summarized his views in a magnificent book called *Disruption* ... which he followed up with another magnificent book called *Beyond Disruption*. Dru claims there are three primary obstacles that keep companies from adopting "disruptive" strategies:

1 Fear of *"cannibalism."* Companies worry that introducing a Cool Product might "confuse" the marketplace and impinge on sales of their current market leaders. (Presumably, as in the case of P&G, even if those "leaders" are declining in sales.)

2 An *"excessive cult of the consumer."* Too great an emphasis on a "customer-driven" approach results in "slavery to demographics, market research and focus groups." Could that old stand-by, "listening to customers," really be the No. 1 sin in marketing? Well, that's more or less what Dru says, and I think he's more or less right. Account planning at ad agencies, says TBWA/Chiat/Day creative director Lee Clow, "has become 'focus group balloting.' "

3 The *"sustainable advantage"* seduction. Sustainable advantage, Dru contends, is a snare, a myth, a delusion. Instead companies should focus on achieving a Current Advantage—and then pray that they can hold onto it long enough to invent something new.

THE CUSTOMER IS ALWAYS LATE
Who wanted Post-it notes? Nobody, for a dozen years. Then they become inevitable. Who wanted fax machines? Nobody, for the longest time. Then a critical mass of "pioneering users" emerged—and traffic began to soar exponentially. Who wanted CDs? Nobody, or at least none of us who had just been through the transition from phonograph records to cassette tapes. Then our kids started using CDs—and we noticed that the quality of the sound was awesome. *Ka-boom.*

The Next Weird Thing

The statistical term "standard deviation" stands for, approximately, *the average difference from the average among a given set of observations*. A "low" standard deviation signals a very "tight" distribution: All the observations are close together. A "high" standard deviation," on the other hand, connotes a very "loose" distribution: The observations are all over the map.

Using this language, I would argue that we are in an Age of High Standard Deviation. All kinds of weird stuff is going on. All kinds of weird competitors are popping up—from terrorists, in the realm of national defense, to upstarts like Dell and Wal*Mart and eBay, in the realm of commerce.

talent

thinking weird

> **WEIRD, "WIDE" STUFF**
>
> *I considered my "weird" argument to be wholly original—that is, until I stumbled across Wayne Burkan's marvelous book* Wide Angle Vision: Beat Your Competition by Focusing on Fringe Competitors, Lost Customers, and Rogue Employees. *In a messy world, Burkan argues, those who lead us to salvation (or at least save us from extinction) will be precisely the kinds of people and enterprises that big companies are wont to dismiss or ignore.*
>
> Burkan writes: "Corporate consciousness is predictably centered around the mainstream. The best customers, biggest competitors, and model employees are almost exclusively the focus of attention."
>
> *This chapter, I gleefully admit, piggybacks off Mr. Burkan's ideas.*

How do we deal with weirdness? Get weird! We need to introduce ... Weirdness in Our Midst. Weird customers. Weird employees. Weird vendors. Weird alliance partners. Weird members on Boards of Directors. And so on.

The main idea, then, is incredibly simple (and, I am quite sure, incredibly powerful): Hang with the dull ...

and you become dull. Dreadfully dull. Hang with the weird ... and you become weird. Wonderfully weird.

I will go way out, to the end of a limb, and argue that Thinking Weird is the *only* surefire strategy for ... Continual Personal Renewal and Radical Organizational Innovation. Now more than ever.

Weird Customers: Always Check the Sell-By Date

"Future-defining customers may account for only two percent to three percent of your total," concedes Adrian Slywotzky of Mercer Management Consulting. But, he adds, "They represent a crucial window on the future." In sum, Slywotzky writes (paraphrasing science-fiction writer William Gibson): "The future has already happened. It's just not evenly distributed."

So what ... EXACTLY ... have you done to insure that your Portfolio of Customers includes "four-sigma weirdos"? I am encouraging you, actually begging you, to measure ... quantitatively ... each customer in that portfolio. ARE THERE ENOUGH FREAKS ON BOARD?

(Warning: If you find yourself unable to sign up freakish customers, then your product or service portfolio really is in trouble!)

DULL CUSTOMERS = DULL YOU.
COOL CUSTOMERS = COOL YOU.

CONSUMER RETORTS (I)
Joseph Morone, president of Bentley College and former dean of RPI business school: "If you worship at the throne of the voice of the customer, you'll get only incremental advances."

CONSUMER RETORTS (II)
Doug Atkin, partner at Merkley Newman Harty: "These days, you can't succeed as a company if you're consumer-led—because, in a world so full of so much constant change, consumers can't anticipate the next big thing. Companies should be *idea*-led and consumer-*informed*."

Weird Competitors: Don't Fence Yourself In

I'm not a fan of "benchmarking." To be sure, I believe in "learning"—from anybody and everybody. And that, I readily admit, is the useful idea behind benchmarking. But here is my (BIG) problem: In nine cases out of ten, benchmarking is done against the "industry leader." A GM (say) measures its supply-chain management practices against (say) Toyota. While I'll acknowledge that Toyota still probably has the drop on GM in supply-chain practices, they aren't the right "benchmark." "Benchmarking" is cool—but only if that benchmark is a truly cool, far-out, four-sigma (six-sigma!?) organization ... doing something wild and wacky and oh-so-2013.

THE GOAL STANDARD

When Jacques Nasser was CEO at Ford, he "benchmarked." And I applauded. Why? His "benchmark" was Dell! That is, a company outside his rather screwed-up industry. Likewise, the U.S. Marine Corps is benchmarking its supply-chain activities against ... Wal*Mart. Hooray!

Arguably, the first noteworthy critic of Benchmarking was none other than Mark Twain. "The best swordsman in the world doesn't need to fear the second best swordsman in the world," Twain wrote. "No, the person for him to be afraid of is some ignorant antagonist who has never had a sword in his hand before; he doesn't do the thing he ought to do, and so the expert isn't prepared for him; he does the thing he ought not to do: and often it catches the expert out and ends him on the spot."

Twain's comment amounts to best analysis I've seen of the problems that beset formerly invincible IBM during the 1980s. Many say that IBM was arrogant and complacent. My contact with the company would support the "arrogant" allegation, but I don't buy the "complacent" bit for a minute. IBM always ... by design ... quaked in its boots. The problem: IBM was quaking over the wrong competitor.

The "invincible" firm had watched "invincible" Detroit humbled by brilliant competitors from Japan and Germany. Hence, as I hung around IBM in the early

1980s, its leaders were mortified by the threats from Germany's Siemens and Japan's Fujitsu. Meanwhile, a bunch of geeky kids—with names like Gates and Jobs—reinvented the industry right out from under IBM's feet. To be sure, IBM made a remarkable recovery during the late 1990s, but its situation was touch-and-go before Lou Gerstner's makeover.

So: How do you keep the truly weird, upstart competitors in the center of your radar screen? How do you spot the next generation of Bill Gateses, Steve Jobses, Charles Schwabs, Ned Johnsons, Michael Dells, and Les Wexners?

Benchmark? Sure! But first, identify the fringe players that are worthy of benchmarking against. Then track them, engage them in joint ventures; perhaps even follow the Cisco-Microsoft-Omnicom Model—and buy them!

DULL COMPETITORS = DULL YOU.
COOL COMPETITORS = COOL YOU.

"IMPOSSIBLE" DREAM
Why is Thinking Weird the … quintessential Talent? Because "If You Can Think Impossible Thoughts, You Can Do Impossible Things."

That's the tag line on the cover of a mind-stretching recent (2004) book: *The Power of Impossible Thinking*, by Yoram (Jerry) Wind and Colin Crook. The authors back up their argument with "hard" research.

Consider this zinger from the prologue:

"Researchers asked subjects to count the number of times ballplayers with white shirts pitched a ball back and forth in a video. Most subjects were so thoroughly engaged in watching white shirts that they failed to notice a black gorilla that wandered across the scene and paused in the middle to beat his chest. They had

their noses so buried in their work that they didn't even see the gorilla.

"What gorillas are moving through your field of vision while you are so hard at work that you fail to see them? Will some of these 800-pound gorillas ultimately disrupt your game?"

In other words: If you can't *see* Weird, you can't *do* Weird.

Are there enough freaks on board?

Weird People: Hire for Latitude

I've never met Craig Venter, but I'm told that he's a bit of a pain. (Some colleagues of his have told me that "a bit" is understatement.) Venter was CEO of Celera Genomics, the upstart that successfully mapped the human genome—and in the process embarrassed the much better-funded Human Genome Project.

I had the opportunity to address the leadership of a giant pharmaceutical company's laboratory. At one point, I queried them, "Do you think that Craig Venter would have come to work for you?"

Few questions, I would contend, are more important: Can you—especially those of you in "established" companies—attract the likes of Craig Venter?

At a business leadership roundtable in London a few years ago, I witnessed an extraordinary exchange. Among those present was an old friend who was a senior professor of business strategy in Sweden. Also in attendance was the top management team of a large, revered Swedish technology company. Perhaps an extra glass of wine or two, or something stronger, was imbibed. At one point, my friend the professor approached the CEO of the "revered" company and said (I remember every word): "I've got about 20 of the sharpest kids in Sweden in my advanced business-strategy seminar. Every one of them tells me he'd sooner die than come to work for you. They're not willing to 'wait their turn' before taking charge of something interesting." There were perhaps 40

of us in the room. My friend hardly boomed his comment. But it was one of those moments: A hush swept the room and you could have heard that proverbial pin drop.

You know what:

MY PAL WAS ON TO SOMETHING! (BIG.)

Established enterprises tend to reject mavericks. Far worse, mavericks wouldn't consider joining them to begin with. Sure, Big Co. has the benefit of "vast resources" and a "vast distribution network." But who the hell cares, if you have to expend 98.6 percent of your youthful energy fighting city hall ... day after day ... week after week ... month after month ... year after year?

LAB TEST

I recall another encounter with a leader from the pharmaceutical industry. This woman, the head of a giant lab, pulled me aside after one of my seminars. "As I was leaving our recent board meeting," she said, "I was accosted by our vice chairman, who once ran R&D. He asked me if I had 'enough weird people' in the labs these days."

One of my hobbies is reading about the history of innovation. While I acknowledge that the issue is complex, I also think there is a rather simple primary lesson: *Innovation Source No.1 is Pissed-Off People.* Anger. That's the source of serious innovation. Which must, of course, be coupled with spine—a willingness to take on the powers that be. And risk it all.

Question: Would Craig Venter come to work for you? Are you able to attract freaks and weirdos and angry world flippers?

Measurement is once again called for: DO YOU HAVE ENOUGH FREAKS AND WEIRDOS ON THE PAYROLL? In Big Co.? In your 28-person HR unit?

DULL EMPLOYEES = DULL YOU.
COOL EMPLOYEES = COOL YOU.

Weird Suppliers: Hey, Big Vendor … Go Away

"Strategic suppliers" has been one of the hottest topics in management over the last decade. Idea: Prune your supplier base from an unwieldy number to a handful with whom you can reliably "partner." Efficiency follows, it is said. And that's usually true.

ANGER MANAGEMENT
Frustration begets innovation. Case I: Mickey Drexler started Gap Kids—because he couldn't find a place to buy decent clothes for his own kid.

Case II: Phil Baechler invented the baby jogger—because he wanted to continue jogging after a baby came into his life. Here's Phil's story: "When Travis was born, I was working a night shift as an editor at the local newspaper. The only way I could get out for my runs during the day was to figure out a way to take him with me. Baby packs sucked, because all they did was bounce him around. Since I was also a former bicycle racer and mechanic, I remembered the early bike trailers and thought it would be great to be able to push him around in some sort of chariot. I got an old stroller, welded a piece of pipe on the back to hold a couple of bike wheels, stuck a Schwinn fork on the front to make it a three wheeler, and we hit the road. … 'Great idea' turned into 'What if?' so I made some prototypes, stuck a mail-order ad in *Runner's World* and it was off to the entrepreneurial (rat) races."

Dull Employees =
DULL YOU
Cool Employees =
COOL YOU

!

So what's the problem? Here's the problem, and it is *enormous:* Strategic suppliers have a principal goal in life relative to you—namely ... SUCKING UP.

I recently spoke to an association of equipment producers that supply a single industry. The good news: They were emerging from the "strategic supplier" revolution. Big customers had decided they wanted to simplify life by getting all their equipment from one or two producers. BIG ONES ... that could offer ... ECONOMIES OF SCALE. Problem: The industry is loaded with dozens of smallish and middle-sized suppliers that are doing seriously innovative things. Since those suppliers were effectively shut out of the big customers' business, they had turned to middle-sized and small-ish customers. Hence, within the supply chain, it was the middle-sized customers, paired with the middle-sized (or smaller) producers, that were introducing the innovative stuff! It took a half-dozen years, but the "big customers" woke up to the fact that they had unintentionally cut themselves off from interesting equipment innovations. As I addressed the group, the tide was reversing. "Strategic supplier" had almost become a contemptuous phrase.

Message: Do you have enough ... Weird Suppliers ... in your portfolio? Or are you too dependent on a small number of Suck-Up (Big) Suppliers?

DULL SUPPLIERS = DULL YOU.

COOL SUPPLIERS = COOL YOU.

Weird Acquisitions:
Buy the Company, Keep the "Change"

I am well known as a Noisy Public Enemy of giant corporate acquisitions. Mating dinosaurs, I have said again and again, is utterly out of step with the times ...

**THEY SUPPLY,
YOU DEMAND**
Wayne Burkan, writing in *Wide Angle Vision:*
"There is an ominous downside to strategic supplier relationships.
[A strategic supplier] is not likely to function as any more than a mirror to your organization. Fringe suppliers that offer innovative business practices need not apply."

which put a premium on speed and nimbleness. But my aversion to dinosaur duos does not make me an enemy of acquisitions per se.

One of the biggest problems at the giant pharmaceutical companies, for example, is the hopelessly complicated drug-discovery processes they've inflicted upon themselves—partly in response to the hopelessly complicated government approval process, partly in response to the increasingly complicated scientific and administrative processes that obtain within companies. In any event, some of the wiser pharma companies have invested significant resources into partnering with, and sometimes acquiring, smaller start-ups. (Pfizer alone is said to have 1,000 such alliances.)

This, I believe, is wise.

Wise ... but not easy to execute. Anything but automatic. Most acquiring giants end up driving away the leaders of the acquired start-ups, even as they give those renegades very sweet compensation packages. They're left with only a shell of their purchase. Cisco Systems (at least when its stock was soaring), the ad giant Omnicom, and damn few others have beaten that rap—by creating post-acquisition environments that give leaders of the acquired firm access to big markets without quashing the entrepreneurial fervor that make a start-up worth buying in the first place.

DULL ACQUISITIONS = DULL YOU.
COOL ACQUISITIONS = COOL YOU.

talent

!

thinking weird

Weird Directors:
Get "Board" Out of Your Skull

All you have to do is look! LOOK AT A DAMN PICTURE OF THE BOARD OF DIRECTORS IN ALMOST ANY ANNUAL REPORT. Old. Old. Old. Tired. Tired. Tired. Unweird. Unweird. Unweird. And frighteningly, hopelessly unrepresentative of the market being served.

Boards matter. (A lot.) So: Appoint weird outsiders to your board!

Ask yourself: Does your Board of Directors include ...

- **At least 30 percent women?**
- **At least one Hispanic?**
- **At least two African-Americans?**
- **A couple of people under the age of 35?**
- **About as many non-U.S. members as your share of non-U.S. sales?**

I am *not* championing "quotas," even if the above reeks thereof. I am championing a board whose composition mirrors the market (which is diverse) and technologies (which are youth-driven) that represent our biggest challenges.

DULL BOARD = DULL YOU.
COOL BOARD = COOL YOU.

BOARDROOM BRAWL?
Yale School of Management prof Jeffrey Sonnenfeld has done research on boards of directors. The upshot: "Weird" wins! Top-performing companies, he concludes, are marked by "extremely contentious boards that regard dissent as an obligation and that treat no subject as undiscussable."

Weird Projects: Measure for Madness

WOW Projects. Weird projects. Same idea, in essence:
You define yourself by your portfolio of projects. Likewise,
your department defines itself by its portfolio of projects.
So: *Is your project portfolio as weird as the times demand?*

All of (enterprise) life comes down to ... your roster
and your portfolio.

Departments *have* people. Departments *do* projects.
That's it. That's all they are ... and that's all they do.

So: Measure your department for ... weirdness.

1. ARE THERE ENOUGH "WEIRD PEOPLE" IN YOUR 26-PERSON TRAINING DEPARTMENT? (ROSTER = PORTFOLIO.) 2. ARE THERE ENOUGH "WEIRD PROJECTS" IN YOUR DEPARTMENT'S PORTFOLIO? (DEPARTMENT = PORTFOLIO OF PROJECTS.)

Idea in detail: You've got 14 active projects; 4 of
them are major. On a strangeness scale (1 = "Polishing
current apples" 10 = "Far out, dude"), how many of
the 14 active projects score 7 or above? Of the 4 major
projects, how many score 6 or above?

DULL PROJECTS = DULL YOU.
COOL PROJECTS = COOL YOU.

talent

!

thinking weird

OVERSIGHT OVERKILL

A Hollywood producer let
me in on a not-so-little
secret about the movie
biz: "Giant projects often
contain within them the
almost certain seeds of
mediocrity. The very fact of
their size causes constant,
microscopic scrutiny
and hence constant
'political' interference.
Such oversight saps the
passion of champions,
and risks—to the point of
certainty—fatal 'dumbing
down' and thence loss of
the very distinction and
quirkiness sought in the
first place."

Weird Encounters: Let's Re-Do "Lunch"

Who did you go to lunch with today? Same-old, same-old? Or some weird new somebody?

Fred Smith, founder and CEO of Federal Express, sat with me on an economic-forecasting panel a few years ago. We chatted a bit before we got going, and at one point he turned on me with a look of determination in his eyes: "Tom, who's the most interesting person you've met in the last 90 days? And how do I get in touch with him or her?" Honestly, that's exactly what he said. Fred was a … Collector of "Weirdos." He wanted to make sure that his business remained a half-dozen years ahead of its vigorous rivals. To have even a chance of doing so, he needed to put himself perpetually in contact with people who were (at least) a half-dozen years ahead of the norm.

How do you do that?

HANG WITH THEM.

Measure (again!): Carefully examine your last 10 business lunches. (Check your calendar. No fudging.) Exactly how many of those lunches have been with newbies (to you) who would score 8 or higher, out of 10, on a Strangeness Scale?

Strangeness is never easy. "Comfortable" is far easier. The problem: "Comfortable" is also well-nigh … USELESS.

These *are* strange times. Strange times call for strange companions.

DULL ENCOUNTERS = DULL YOU.

COOL ENCOUNTERS = COOL YOU.

talent

thinking weird

TALENT: YOU KNOW IT WHEN YOU (CAN'T) SEE IT

Thinking Weird is a … preeminent talent. It is also, ever so importantly, an intangible *talent. In this age of Value-Added Intellectual Capital— when value derives less from solid lumps than from weightless ideas— the key to talent is usually something that you can't … put a finger on.*

Below is a list of intangible attributes that mark "talent" as, well, Talent. A true exemplar of "talent" …

:-0   **DISPLAYS PASSION.** *There are enthusiasts … those who are visibly energetic and passionate about everything. And there are those who are not. Be among the enthusiasts.*

:·●   **INSPIRES OTHERS.** *Inspirational ability is elusive. The best test:* Does this person inspire me?

;-)   **LOVES PRESSURE.** *One reason former athletes tend to do relatively well in leadership positions: They have been tested in a cauldron of chaos—for instance, in the last two minutes of a football game. These are often folks who blather and bumble when things are calm—and then come into their … Awesome Own … when mess and mayhem occur.*

:·)'   **CRAVES ACTION.** *Former Honeywell boss Larry Bossidy says that he interviews two kinds of people. Those who talk about "vision and philosophy." And those who talk about the Grubby Details of the Stuff That They've Gotten Done … and the Barriers They've Smashed to Get It Done. Be one of the latter—an action fanatic.*

:-D   **KNOWS HOW TO FINISH THE JOB.** *A lot of folks are great at the "first 98 percent" … but fail to "tidy up" the "political loose ends" (or whatever) that are the Essence of Implementation with Impact. Be a "last two percent" person.*

:·]   **THRIVES ON WOW.** *A true "talent" has a fat "WOW Projects" Portfolio—and loves to talk about … Projects that Flew in the Face of Conventional Wisdom. Efforts that "took on" the bureaucracy. Jobs that nobody else wanted that resulted in Gems of Achievement.*

;-/   **EXHIBITS CURIOSITY.** *There are those who …* Don't Ask Questions. *And there are those who …* Can't Stop Asking Question*s. Be known as an Asker of Questions.*

:0)   **EXUDES A SENSE OF FUN.** *The greatest "catch" for any employer or team leader is the world-beater with a "twinkle in the eye." The performance fanatic who also has a knack for creating a spirited environment. This quality is as valuable in a 23-year-old recruit as it is in a Senior Officer.*

:-}   **THINKS AT A HIGH LEVEL.** *Is intelligence "all-important"? No, not compared with other attributes listed here. (Raw smarts is not even close to the top, as I see it.) But the challenging nature of business today does require a decent degree of intelligence.*

talent

thinking weird

Weird Ideas: How to Achieve "Sutton" Impact

For a matchless exposition of the Power of Weird, inhale Bob Sutton's book *Weird Ideas That Work: 11½ Practices for Promoting, Managing, and Sustaining Innovation*.

Here, in summary, are his 11-plus strange practices:

1. Hire slow learners (of the organizational code).

1.5 Hire people who make you uncomfortable, even those you dislike.

2. Hire people you (probably) don't need.

3. Use job interviews to get ideas, not (just) to screen candidates.

4. Encourage people to ignore and defy superiors as well as peers.

5. Find some happy people and get them to fight.

6. Reward success and failure, punish inaction.

7. Decide to do something that will probably fail, then convince yourself and everyone else that success is certain.

8. Think of some ridiculous, impractical things to do, then do them.

9. Avoid, distract, and bore customers, critics, and anyone who just wants to talk about money.

10. Don't try to learn anything from people who seem to have solved the problems you face.

11. Forget the past—particularly your company's past success.

DULL PRACTICES = DULL YOU.

COOL PRACTICES = COOL YOU.

SUTTON DEPTH

I love Bob Sutton's Weird Ideas That Work. *But even more, I am head-over-heels in love with the fact that such a book even exists, and that it was written by a Tenured Professor of Industrial Engineering at no less than Stanford University. Are we finally reaching a point where "strange ideas" are deemed ... not so strange?*

For more on how "weird ideas ... work," see the Cool Friends interview with Sutton, page 128.

The Obsolescence of "Planning"

Those 11½ Weird Ideas, I think, could almost be reduced to one:

FIRE THE PLANNERS. HIRE THE FREAKS.

We don't need elaborate plans! There is no time to plan! WE NEED ACTION! WE NEED HEROES!

Heroes ... freaks ... people who have the nerve to stand up, stick out, and fight conventional wisdom.

These are "weird times." Therefore, we must think "weird." Forget "plans." Forget "processes." Instead: Focus on finding a host of New Exemplars ... folks whom you can ferret out of the boondocks and parade before their peers as ... New Culture Carriers.

DULL MATES = DULL YOU.
COOL MATES = COOL YOU.

talent

!

thinking weird

Of Ships and Fools: Brute Force, Brave Freaks

Real innovation is all about ... FORCE. Forcing yourself into contact with those who will force *you* to move in a direction that is significantly different from your prior path to success.

FROM "GOOD" TO ...
CRAZY

Hajime Mitarai, CEO of Canon: "We should do something when people say it is 'crazy.' If people say something is 'good,' it means that someone else is already doing it."

FROM CRAZY TO ...
CRAZIER!

Nobel-awarded physicist Niels Bohr reportedly once said to fellow physicist Wolfgang Pauli: "We are all agreed that your theory is crazy. The question, which divides us, is whether it's crazy enough."

Operational suggestion: When you're considering a course of action at your next project meeting, ask yourself and the group, "Is it crazy enough?"

CRAZY THOUGHT?

Jeffrey Pfeffer, professor at Stanford Graduate School of Business, speaking in 2004: "There is little evidence that mastery of the knowledge acquired in business schools enhances people's careers, or that even attaining the MBA credential itself has much effect on graduates' salaries or career attainment."

One thing is certain: You won't learn to Think Weird at most B-schools.

The ultimate exponent of that approach was an explorer. Hernando Cortez. As the story goes, Cortez landed with his hearty band of soldiers in Veracruz, Mexico. They headed inland. They faced disease, brutal living conditions, and a resolute enemy. Fearing that the soldiers might flag in their determination to keep going, Cortez resorted to a brutal, beautifully simple remedy: He burned the ships that could have taken the soldiers home.

BURN THE SHIPS. Now, that is a Bold Strategy.

Question: HAVE YOU "BURNED YOUR SHIPS"? HAVE YOU DUMPED ANY OF THE ONES WHO BRUNG YOU?

In practical terms, "burning your ships" means ... cleansing your portfolio of its "successful" yesterdays. There are companies out there—even Big Companies— that "get it."

- Hewlett-Packard sold off several divisions that were the founding pillars of the company.
- 3M sold off several divisions that were the founding pillars of the company.
- Corning sold off several divisions that were the founding pillars of the company.
- Nokia sold off virtually all the literal founding pillars (that is, trees) of the company.

How do you put yourself in a "ship-burning" state of mind? Simple:

FIND THE FREAKS!

SIGN 'EM UP!

LISTEN TO 'EM!

TAKE 'EM INTO YOUR CONFIDENCE!

MAKE 'EM YOUR PARTNERS!

LET 'EM HELP YOU MAKE REVOLUTION!

WE HAVE IGNITION
Jack Kerouac, writing in *On the Road*: "The only people for me are the mad ones, the ones who are mad to live, mad to talk, mad to be saved, desirous of everything at the same time, the ones who never yawn or say a commonplace thing, but burn, burn, burn like fabulous yellow roman candles exploding like spiders across the stars."

GRAVEYARD SHIFT
There is a wretched old saying in the world of science: "If you want a paradigm shift, it's not good enough for the old professors to retire. They must die."

A little strong? No doubt. However: I BELIEVE IT.

TOP 10 TO-DOs

1. *Sell Weird.* Cultivate customers whose "weird" demands will propel you into the Freaky Future of your industry. What they lack in profitability, they more than make up for in … *prophecy.*

2. *Compete Weird.* Look far beyond your "natural" competitive set. Ask not "Who are we competing against?" … but "Who is (or will be, or wants to be) competing against *us*—whether we know it or not?"

3. *Hire Weird.* Fill your ranks with people who are too Teed-Off to Toe the Line. In other words: Hire *angry.*

4. *Buy Weird.* Prune your supplier list of "strategic suppliers" whose strategy amounts to blocking your access to True Innovation.

5. *Acquire Weird.* Use mergers and acquisitions not to Get Big … but to Get Weird. Buy only those companies that will force you out of your comfort zone. (And please: Don't force them *into* that zone.)

6. *Govern Weird.* Spice your Board of Directors with a diverse array of mold-breaking types. I *hate* quotas. I *love* doing whatever it takes to create a board that is Weird enough for these Weird Times.

7. *Measure Weird.* Shake up the metrics that you use to rate people and projects. Make it official: Create a "W" score, for example, that lets you rank projects according to their Weird Potential.

8. *Meet Weird.* Schedule *(today!)* three lunch dates with people who strike you as strange … who embarrass you … who *scare* you.

9. *Think Weird.* Consult Robert Sutton's "11½ Weird Ideas That Work." Plan to act on at least 6⅔ of those ideas. (Don't know how to "act on" "⅔" of an idea? Obviously, you're not Weird enough yet!)

10. *Work Weird.* Every day remind yourself (put it on a 3x5 card that you carry everywhere) that success derives from Talent … and Talent derives from working along the twin axes of WOW and Weird.

INDEX

AUTHOR'S ACKNOWLEDGMENTS

It required a far-flung virtual village to make this book. Here I wish to note a few "essential" residents of that village:

Michael Slind, editor, and Jason Godfrey, designer, both continued the sterling work that helped make my previous book (*Re-imagine!*) so sharply compelling. In adapting that book to make this one, they both achieved the noble feat of reinventing the project from within.

Stephanie Jackson, of Dorling Kindersley, pushed and pushed—and charmed and charmed—this book into being. Also at DK, Peter Luff used his sense of visual panache to help produce a "small" book with big impact, and Dawn Henderson applied her editorial talent deftly, creatively, and crucially at every stage of the project.

Erik Hansen served in his usual role of "project manager," though that term fails to capture the unique mix of doggedness and nimbleness that he brings to all of my publishing ventures. Cathy Mosca attended to details of authorial execution and factual accuracy with her typical vigilance.

My thanks to them all.

FOR THE CURIOUS ...
Source notes on the stories and data cited in this book are available online (www.tompeters.com/essentials/notes. php). Also on the Web are complete versions of the Cool Friends interviews excerpted in the book (www.tompeters. com/cool_friends/friends.php).

PICTURE CREDITS

Picture Researcher : Sarah Hopper
DK Picture Library : Richard Dabb

The publisher would like to thank the following for their kind permission to reproduce their photographs;
(Abbreviations key; t=top, b=below, r=right, l=left, c=centre, a=above, tl=top left, tr=top right, bl=below left, br=below right).

10: Getty Images/Ellen Stagg; 14: Corbis/ Jim Craigmyle (b); 15: ArenaPAL (tc), Corbis/Chris Trotman (tl), Corbis/Howard Keline (bl), Corbis/Kraig Geiger (tr), Corbis/Steven E. Sutton (bc), Ronald Grant Archive/Twentieth Century Fox (br); 21: Getty Images/Tim Simmons; 27: Getty Images/Walter Hodges; 29: The Art Archive (t), The Art Archive/National Archives, Washington D.C. (b); 32: www.bridgeman. co.uk/Fenimore Art Museum, Cooperstown, NY; 37: Corbis/Gary Houlder; 38: Getty Images/ Warren Bolster; 41: Zefa Visual Media/Mika; 44: Corbis/Lito C.Uyan; 54: Getty Images/Ellen Stagg; 59: Science Photo Library/NASA; 60: Corbis/E.O.Hoppe (b), Topfoto.co.uk/2005 UPP (t); 67: Left Lane Productions/Corbis; 74: Getty Images/Ellen Stagg; 78: Corbis/Bettmann (b); 82: Corbis/Marco Cristofori; 85: DK Images/Gift of Rolodex Corporation/ Cooper Hewitt Museum; 88: Science Photo Library/Colin Cuthbert; 92: Corbis/ Bettmann; 102: Getty Images/Ellen Stagg; 115: Corbis/Bruce Miller (b); 120-121: Corbis/Anthony Redpath; 122: Corbis/Doug Wilson; 126: Getty Images/Shannon Fagan; 135: Getty Images/Martin Barraud; 137: Getty Images/Bruce Laurance; 141: Corbis; 142: Corbis/Anthony Redpath (tc), Corbis/ Bettmann (tr), Corbis/Larry Hirshowitz (tl); 143: Corbis/Peter M.Fisher (tc), Getty Images/Jana Leon (tr), Getty Images/Peter Beavis (tl); 144: Corbis/Patrick Ward; 150: Corbis/Didier Robcis.

All other images © Dorling Kindersley.
For further information see:
www.dkimages.com

Hear Tom Peters Live with Red Audio (TM).

ABOUT THE AUTHOR

The Economist *called Tom Peters the Uber-guru.* BusinessWeek *labelled him "business's best friend and worst nightmare."* Fortune *tagged him as the Ur-guru of management, and compared him to Ralph Waldo Emerson, Henry David Thoreau, Walt Whitman, and H.L. Mencken. In an in-depth study released by Accenture's Institute for Strategic Change in 2002, he scored second among the top 50 "Business Intellectuals," behind Michael Porter and ahead of Peter Drucker.*

In 2004 the compilers of Movers and Shakers: The Brains and Bravado Behind Business *reviewed the contributions of 100 business thinkers and practitioners, from Machiavelli to J.P. Morgan to Jack Welch. Here's how the book summarized Tom's impact: "Tom Peters has probably done more than anyone else to shift the debate on management from the confines of boardrooms, academia, and consultancies to a broader, worldwide audience, where it has become the staple diet of the media and managers alike. Peter Drucker has written more and his ideas have withstood a longer test of time, but it is Peters—as consultant, writer, columnist, seminar lecturer, and stage performer—whose energy, style, influence, and ideas have shaped new management thinking."*

Tom's first book, coauthored with Robert J. Waterman, was In Search of Excellence *(1982). National Public Radio in 1999 placed the book among the "Top Three Business Books of the Century," and a poll by Bloomsbury Publishing in 2002 ranked it as the "greatest business book of all time." Tom followed* Search *with a string of international best-sellers:* A Passion for Excellence *(1985, with Nancy Austin),* Thriving on Chaos *(1987),* Liberation Management *(1992),* The Tom Peters Seminar: Crazy Times Call for Crazy Organizations *(1993),* The Pursuit of WOW! *(1994);* The Circle of Innovation: You Can't Shrink Your Way to Greatness *(1997), and a series of books on Reinventing Work—*The Brand You50, The Project50, *and* The Professional Service Firm50 *(1999). In 2003 Tom joined with publisher Dorling Kindersley to release* Re-imagine! Business Excellence in a Disruptive Age. *That book, which aims to reinvent the business book through energetic presentation of critical ideas, immediately became an international No.1 bestseller.*

Leadership guru Warren Bennis, the only person who knows both Tom and Peter Drucker first-hand, told a reporter, "If Peter Drucker invented modern management, Tom Peters vivified it." Indeed, throughout his career, Tom's overriding passion has been passion. Among his current passions: women as leaders; the supreme role of design in product and service differentiation; the creation of customer experiences that rival a Cirque du Soleil performance; and the enormous, underserved markets represented by women and by Boomers.

Born in Baltimore in 1942, Tom resided in Northern California from 1974 to 2000 and now lives on a 1,600-acre working farm in Vermont with his wife, Susan Sargent. He has degrees in civil engineering from Cornell University (B.C.E., M.C.E.) and in business from Stanford University (M.B.A., Ph.D.). He holds honorary doctorates from several institutions, including the State University of Management in Moscow (2004). Serving in the U.S. Navy from 1966 to 1970, he made two deployments to Vietnam (as a Navy Seabee) and survived a tour in the Pentagon. He also served as a senior White House drug-abuse advisor from 1973 to 1974. From 1974 to 1981, he worked at McKinsey & Co., becoming a partner and Organization Effectiveness practice leader in 1979. Tom is a Fellow of the International Academy of Management, the World Productivity Association, the International Customer Service Association, and the Society for Quality and Participation. Today, he presents about 75 major seminars each year (half of them outside the United States), and participates in numerous other learning events, both in person and on the Web.

SAY IT LOUD – THE ESSENTIALS MANIFESTO

They say...   I say...

They say...	I say...
Sure, we need "change."	We need REVOLUTION. NOW.
Your (my) language is extreme.	The times are extreme.
I am extreme.	I am a realist.
I demand too much.	"They" accept mediocrity too readily.
Brand You is not for everyone.	The alternative is unemployment.
Take a deep breath. Be calm.	Tell it to Wal*Mart. Tell it to China. Tell it to India. Tell it to Dell. Tell it to Microsoft.
What's wrong with a "good product"?	Wal*Mart or China or both are about to eat your lunch. Why can't you provide instead a Fabulous Experience?
The Web is a "useful tool."	The Web changes everything. Now.
We need an "initiative."	We need a Dream. And Dreamers.
Great Design is nice.	Great Design is mandatory.
You (I) overplay the "women's thing."	The minuscule share of Women in Senior Leadership Positions is a Waste and a Disgrace and a Strategic Marketing Error.
We need a "project" to explore "new markets."	We need Total Strategic Realignment to exploit the Women and Boomer markets.
"Wow" is "typical Tom."	"WOW" is a Minimum Survival Requirement.
We like people who, with steely determination, say, "I can make it better."	I love people who, with a certain maniacal gleam in their eye, perhaps even a giggle, say, "I can turn the world upside-down!"
Let's speed things up.	Let's transform the Corporate Metabolism until Insane Urgency becomes a Sacrament.
We want recruits with "spotless records."	Those "spots" are what defines Talent.
We favor a "team" that works in "harmony."	Give me a raucous brawl among the most creative people imaginable.
We want "happy" customers.	Give me pushy, needy, nasty, provocative customers who will drag me down Innovation Boulevard at 100mph.
We want to partner with "best of breed."	Give me Coolest of Breed.
Happy balance.	Creative Tension.
Peace, brother.	Bruise my feelings. Flatten my ego. SAVE MY JOB.
Plan it.	DO IT.
Market share.	Market Creation.
Basic black.	TECHNICOLOR RULES!
Conglomerate and Imitate.	Create and Innovate.
Improve and Maintain.	DESTROY and RE-IMAGINE!